Women
of the Wind

EARLY WOMEN AVIATORS

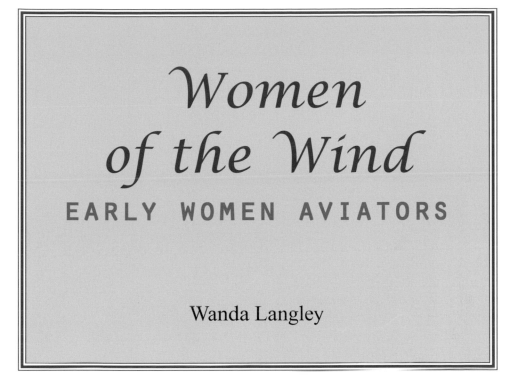

Women of the Wind

EARLY WOMEN AVIATORS

Wanda Langley

MORGAN
REYNOLDS
PUBLISHING

Greensboro, North Carolina

Ynes Mexia

Women of the Sea

Women of the Wind

Women
Adventurers

WOMEN OF THE WIND: EARLY WOMEN AVIATORS

Library of Congress Cataloging-in-Publication Data

Langley, Wanda.
    Women of the wind : early women aviators / Wanda Langley.
        p. cm.
Includes bibliographical references and index.
    ISBN-13: 978-1-931798-81-5 (library binding)
    ISBN-10: 1-931798-81-8 (library binding)
    1. Women air pilots—United States—Biography—Juvenile literature. 2.
Air pilots—United States—Biography—Juvenile literature. I. Title.
    TL539.L28 2006
    629.13'092'273—dc22
                                        2005022951

Printed in the United States of America
First Edition

To Charles and Jonathan,
who appreciate strong women

contents

Harriet Quimby. (Library of Congress)

Harriet Quimby

THE COLORFUL BIRDWOMAN

Harriet Quimby started something. Eight years after the Wright brothers first flew their plane in North Carolina in 1903, Quimby became the first woman in America to earn her pilot's license. She showed the new world of aviation that women could fly planes, and soon other female fliers followed her.

Harriet Quimby was born May 11, 1875, to a farm family in Coldwater, Michigan. When Harriet was nine, the family moved to California. She, her mother, and her older sister sewed prune sacks for the fruit-packing industry. Harriet and her mother also mixed and bottled her uncle's herbal formulas, while her father sold the medicines from a wagon. Harriet's mother, who believed that women were equal to men (a radical notion in those days), greatly influenced her.

At the age of twenty-six, Harriet Quimby became a reporter for a San Francisco newspaper. She decided to move east to advance her writing career and, in 1903, landed a job in New York as a drama critic for *Leslie's Illustrated Weekly,* a popular magazine of the time.

In 1910, thirty-five-year-old Quimby fell in love with airplanes. It happened on an October day at the Belmont Park Air Meet on Long Island, New York, where she first saw these strange sky machines. She watched the pilots—"birdmen-heroes," as she described them—making loops and dives. She decided she had to fly.

Quimby saw her writing as a way to publicize the new air age. She wanted to dispel the myth that planes were too difficult for women to fly. She later wrote, "In my opinion, there is no reason why the aeroplane should not open up a fruitful occupation for women. I see no reason why they cannot realize handsome incomes by carrying passengers between adjacent towns, why they cannot derive incomes from parcel delivery, from taking photographs from above, or from conducting schools for flying."

With Quimby on that day was her good friend Matilde Moisant. One of the dashing fliers was Moisant's brother John, who had raced that day from Long Island to the Statue of Liberty and back. Quimby was so inspired that when she saw John at dinner that evening, she asked him to teach her to fly, and he agreed. But before the lessons could begin, he was killed during an air show in New Orleans. His death did not dampen Quimby's enthusiasm for flying.

Harriet Quimby (right) *and Matilde Moisant in 1911, shortly after they learned to fly.* (Smithsonian Institution)

In April 1911, Quimby and Matilde Moisant signed up as students at the Moisant School of Aviation, started by John and his brother Alfred. Because most male fliers thought women could not—or should not—fly, Harriet and Matilde went to the airfield disguised as men. They started their lessons on May 10.

Quimby took her flying sessions at sunrise because the air was calmer then. Her French flight instructor gave her lessons on a Blériot thirty-horsepower monoplane, a French plane with one set of wings. Each lesson in the air lasted two to five minutes (the accepted length of flight instruction in the French aeronautical schools) and cost $2.50 a minute.

After thirty-three lessons over a two-month period, Quimby decided to try to qualify for her pilot's license. She would be the first American woman to attempt this feat. (In 1910, Baroness Raymonde de la Roche of France had become the first woman to earn a pilot's license.) Pilots were not required to obtain licenses in order to fly, but Quimby wanted to be the first woman in the United States to hold this distinction.

In order to get a license, early pilots had to complete a three-part flight test: make five right and left alternating turns around a tall pole called a pylon; fly five figure eights; and land the plane within one hundred feet of a white square that marked the spot where the plane started. This flight test had to be witnessed by two judges from the Aero Club of America.

On the last day of July 1911, Quimby climbed into her

Quimby became the first American woman to receive a pilot's license after successfully completing her flight test in her Blériot on August 1, 1911. (Library of Congress)

Blériot plane. She successfully completed the first two requirements, but she landed too far from the designated spot. She had to wait until the next day to make another attempt.

Word soon spread that a woman was trying for her pilot's license. The following day, August 1, a crowd gathered to witness the event. Quimby lifted off, flying about 150 feet off the ground and going forty-five miles an hour. She circled the airfield, then descended for the landing. When the wheels touched the ground, she shut her motor off in order to stop because the plane had no brakes. She landed her plane exactly seven feet, nine inches from where she had started. Castor oil, used as a lubricant on the engine, covered her face.

Quimby described what happened next: "I removed my goggles, then climbed out of my monoplane. The crowd was applauding and it sounded good to me. I waved to everybody and nonchalantly walked over to the official observer. I looked him in the eye and said, well I guess I get my license. I guess you do, the man replied."

On August 2, 1911, the Aero Club issued a pilot's license to Harriet Quimby. Her certificate read No. 37, meaning she was the thirty-seventh American to receive a pilot's license. Twelve days later, Matilde Moisant received her license, becoming the second American woman to do so.

The Moisant International Aviators, an exhibition team, invited Quimby and Matilde to join. The two began performing almost immediately. In September 1911, Quimby participated in a Staten Island air meet in New York, where she made a moonlight flight. Twenty thousand spectators cheered for her. She earned $1,500 for her performance. Later that month, she entered the Nassau Boulevard Meet in New York, where she raced— and beat—the celebrated French aviator Hélène Dutrieu. Quimby and Matilde Moisant attracted much attention when they did an aerial show at the inauguration of Mexico's new president, Francisco Madero.

Everywhere, crowds went wild over Quimby. She stood out from the rest of the aviators, not only because she was a woman but also because of her colorful flying outfit. She had a tailor make her a one-piece flying suit of plum-colored satin, backed with wool for warmth. She wore the trousers tucked into high-laced boots and

Quimby poses in her purple flying suit.
(Library of Congress)

topped off her garb with a monk-like hood and a pair of streamlined goggles.

Quimby was as colorful as her flying suit. The tall, green-eyed beauty always dressed with great style. Her outgoing personality attracted many friends. And she loved publicity. She led people to believe that she was born to a wealthy California family and had attended private schools in Europe and America. She also told people she was ten years younger than her actual age.

Nine months after she received her license in 1911, Quimby decided she wanted to be the first woman to fly across the English Channel—and she wanted to become famous doing it. As a drama critic, Quimby understood the importance of planning, publicity, and the dramatic moment.

However, the colorful birdwoman was not all show. She was a serious and careful pilot. Before each flight, Quimby studied her routine, knew what her plane could do, and worked closely with her mechanic and manager. She wrote, "Only a cautious person—man or woman—should fly. I never mount my [plane] until every wire and screw has been tested."

Quimby knew what she needed to do to make the dangerous twenty-two-mile flight across the English Channel. She planned it all carefully. First, she hired a business manager, Leo Stevens, and the two traveled to London where they arranged financing for the flight. She sold the right to her story of the crossing to a London newspaper, the *Daily Mirror*. She also talked an English businessman into paying her $5,000 if the flight were successful.

Quimby and Stevens then went to Paris to order the plane. She purchased a Blériot XI, a fifty-horsepower aircraft. The plane was designed by Louis Blériot, a Frenchman who had made the first crossing of the English Channel in 1909. The Blériot was a monoplane with one set of wings. Crafted of wood, canvas, and wire, it had an open body and bicycle-like wheels. Its joystick was the controlling lever. The pilot's feet rested on a steering bar, which was connected to the rudder by wires. The plane had no brakes.

High winds prevented a test flight in France, so Quimby went to Dover, England, to wait for her plane to be delivered. While there, news came that another woman

This cigar-box label commemorates aviator and airplane designer Louis Blériot, the first person to fly across the English Channel. (Library of Congress)

had crossed the English Channel by plane. English-woman Eleanor Trehawke Davis had flown across on April 2, 1912—but she had flown as a passenger. Gustav Hamel, a famous English aviator, had piloted the flight. Undaunted, Quimby and her business manager promptly hired Hamel as adviser and proceeded with their plans.

Hamel thought the English Channel was too danger-ous for Quimby to cross so he offered to fly for her. He proposed donning her satin flying suit, landing in an isolated spot on the French coast, and giving the suit to a waiting Quimby. She could climb into the plane, wait to be found, and claim the glory of being the first woman to fly across the English Channel. Quimby refused his offer, although she did let him instruct her in using a compass.

When Quimby's plane arrived in England, the weather was too bad for her to test her new aircraft. She would have to test it during the flight. On Sunday, April 14, the day dawned clear. But Quimby refused to take off because she had promised her religious father she would never fly on a Sunday. Foul weather closed in again the following day.

In the early morning hours of Tuesday, April 16, the wind was calm. However, a fogbank lay across the Channel. After discussing the situation with her manager and ground crew, Quimby decided she would go. She put a long woolen coat over her satin flying suit. She topped that with a raincoat and a sealskin stole. Long, woolen gloves covered her hands. Fearing Quimby would still get cold, Hamel tied a hot water bottle around her waist. The monoplane was hurried out of the hanger.

Gustav Hamel helps Quimby prepare in the last minutes before taking off to cross the English Channel on April 16, 1912. (Smithsonian Institution)

It was now 5:30 AM. Six men held down the plane while Hamel helped Quimby into the wicker chair in the open cockpit. The mechanic pulled down hard on the propeller and the engine fired twice, sending oily smoke over everyone. Hamel shouted, "Good luck!" and jumped off the wing. Quimby gave the signal, and the ground crew let the plane go. It bumped along the ground, gathering speed, until it was airborne. Soaring, the Blériot looked like a giant wooden dragonfly held together with wire.

Quimby headed over Dover Castle so the *Daily Mirror*'s photographers and moving-picture men could take her picture, as promised. She flew over the white cliffs of Dover and was soon over open water. Fog enveloped her, and she could see neither the water below nor the French coast ahead. Her goggles fogged over, so she pushed them up on her forehead.

She pulled the plane up, trying to get above the thick fogbank. Despite her layers of clothing and the hot water bottle, she shivered. Quimby focused on her compass, jammed between her knees. She had to fly a straight course. If she veered off by just five miles, she would find herself over the North Sea. She concentrated on keeping the plane on an even keel.

When going over the fogbank didn't work, Quimby descended, trying to get under it. The plane started to tilt, causing the engine to flood and misfire. Quimby prepared herself to pancake down on the water. Fortunately, the excess gasoline burned off, and the engine resumed its steady, hammering beats. At one thousand feet, Quimby leveled off. She managed to get under the cloud cover and now could see the French coast. She flew about a mile a minute. The sun shone directly in her eyes. She headed toward the white beaches but could not see the town of Calais.

Quimby set the plane down on the beach. She had missed Calais by about twenty-five miles. No matter— she had crossed the English Channel. People from a nearby fishing village ran to greet her and carried her on their shoulders into town. She caught a train into

The English Channel separates the southern coast of England from northwest France.

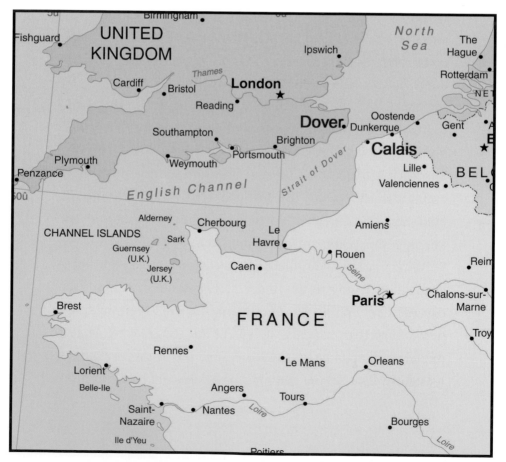

Paris, where she was acclaimed for her successful endeavor. Quimby looked forward to seeing herself in all the American newspapers.

But the next day the papers carried news of greater importance. As Quimby had prepared for her Channel flight, during the night of April 14-15, 1912, a giant ocean liner had hit an iceberg in the North Atlantic. Stories about the horrible tragedy filled the American newspapers. Harriet Quimby's historic flight had been knocked off the front pages of the newspapers by the sinking of the *Titanic.*

In May, she returned to New York and resumed her post at *Leslie's Illustrated.* Just a month later, she showed up at the Boston Air Meet flying a new all-white, seventy-horsepower Blériot. It was a beautiful two-seated plane, but it was also tricky to fly and tended to be unstable in the air. Other women pilots participated in the meet, including Matilde Moisant and Blanche Scott, the first American woman to fly an airplane in 1910. Another young aspiring woman pilot, Ruth Law, observed the air show that day.

On July 1, 1912, Quimby and a passenger, William Willard, lifted off in late afternoon. They flew over Dorchester Bay, rounded Boston Light, then circled over the airfield. The flight lasted about twenty minutes. Quimby descended from 3,000 to 1,000 feet over the bay, going about eighty-five miles an hour. Neither wore a seat belt. (It is unclear whether the plane had seat belts.) Suddenly the plane went into a dive, and Willard was catapulted from his seat. The Blériot then flipped over, and Quimby was ejected. Horrified spectators could only stand by helplessly. Rescuers pulled the two bodies out of five feet of water, but it was too late: Quimby and Willard had died from broken backs. The plane, however, glided to a landing with little damage.

Inspectors examined Harriet's aircraft to see why it fell from the sky. They came up with several possible theories: Willard had shifted his weight, upsetting the plane's balance; a sudden gust of wind had caught the unstable Blériot; it had hit an air pocket; or the pilot had come in too fast. The experts could not determine the exact cause of the accident.

Quimby's aviation achievements—including the English Channel crossing—finally made the front pages of the New York newspapers. Americans mourned the death of Harriet Quimby, the colorful birdwoman who fell from the sky.

TIMELINE

1875	Born in Coldwater, Michigan, on May 11.
1902	Becomes a journalist for San Francisco, California, newspapers.
1903	Moves to New York and writes for *Leslie's Illustrated Weekly.*
1911	Takes first flight lesson in May; receives pilot's license in August; makes night flight over Staten Island, New York, in September; joins Moisant International Aviators as an exhibition pilot.
1912	Becomes first woman to pilot a plane across the English Channel on April 16; dies in plane crash in Boston, Massachusetts, on July 1.
1991	Honored on U.S. postage stamp.

Katherine Stinson. (Library of Congress)

Katherine Stinson

THE FLYING SCHOOLGIRL

Katherine Stinson's mother never told her, "Be careful, now. Don't do that. You might get hurt." Emma Stinson did not say it when Katherine abandoned concert piano training in 1912 to take up flying. She did not even say it when her daughter performed dangerous stunts in the sky. But Katherine was never seriously hurt—and she was never afraid when she flew.

Katherine Stinson was born February 14, 1891, in Ft. Payne, Alabama, the eldest among four remarkable children: herself, sister Marjorie, and brothers Jack and Eddie. All became fliers. Their parents divorced in 1904, and Emma Stinson reared the children on her own.

Growing up, Katherine excelled at the piano and dreamed of becoming a concert pianist. However, she

Hot-air balloon travel, developed in the late eighteenth century, was one of the only ways for humans to experience air travel before the Wright brothers' successful flight in 1903. (Library of Congress)

would have to go to Europe for further study. This would take more money than the family had. When she read that exhibition fliers (also called barnstormers) earned up to $1,000 a week, she thought that would be a way to get the money she needed. But first, she had to find out whether she had any fear in the air.

On August 31, 1911, Katherine Stinson took her first flight in a hot-air balloon in Kansas City, Missouri. Delighted with the sereneness and freedom of the sky, she thought she could learn to fly airplanes. Stinson sold her piano for $200 and borrowed another $300 from her father for flying lessons. If she could earn $1,000 a week, she could soon buy another piano and fund her studies in Europe.

Stinson went to a flight school in St. Louis, Missouri, and had her first plane ride on January 21, 1912. In an effort to scare her, the pilot climbed to 1,000 feet and banked the plane. When they landed twenty minutes later, Stinson was more eager to fly than ever. She took a few lessons and impressed her flight instructor with her natural aptitude. However, the owner thought that this five-foot-tall, hundred-pound woman would crash his plane. He did not want her on his flying field.

Undaunted, Stinson left for Chicago, Illinois, for more flying lessons. In May 1912, she began her flight training at Max Lillie's flying school. Lillie did not have a problem with Stinson's small size because she proved to be quick, dexterous, and possessed of great calm-ness—qualities needed to become a good pilot.

Like most pilots of that era, Stinson learned to fly in a Wright B plane, with a thirty- to thirty-five-horse-power engine. The frame was made of spruce wood, and muslin fabric covered the wings. Wires and vertical wooden poles, called struts, held the upper and lower wings together. The Wright B looked like a rectangular box kite in the air.

To fly this plane, a pilot had to operate two levers, or "joysticks." The left joystick controlled the elevators on the horizontal wings of the tail, which made the plane go up or down. The right joystick moved from side to side, causing the plane to roll. While performing, pilots had to use these controls simultaneously, all the while watching the ground and the horizon. They also had to keep an eye on weather conditions and watch out for hazardous objects, such as birds. Flying such a difficult, dangerous aircraft was not for the faint of heart.

On July 13, 1912, Stinson soloed; three days later, she passed her qualifying test. She received her pilot's license (No. 148) on July 24, 1912. It would not be long before Katherine Stinson would abandon her dream of a career as a concert pianist. She would make her living—and her name—by flying.

In 1913, Stinson bought a Wright B plane from Max Lillie for $2,000. Before she flew the plane, she scrubbed it thoroughly, much to the amusement of the male mechanics. When she removed the grime and grease, she discovered frayed wires that could have broken while in flight, causing the plane to crash. Stinson made a career-long habit of always maintaining her plane and carefully inspecting it before each flight.

The Wright B Flyer was originally designed to provide pilot training and reconnaissance for the U.S. Army Signal Corps. (Library of Congress)

The new aviator began her career in 1913 in grand flying style. On New Year's Day, she flew a rose-covered plane in the Rose Bowl Parade in Pasadena, California. She spent the summer barnstorming in the Midwest and the South. Between September 23 and 27, Stinson carried 1,333 pieces of mail during the Montana State Fair, becoming the first woman authorized to carry the U.S. mail by air. She ended the year by flying over London, England, in December.

In April 1913, she founded and became president of the Stinson Aviation Company. Her mother assumed the role of secretary/treasurer of the company. Stinson earned money for the company by doing exhibition flying. She gave her siblings rides in her plane and inspired them to fly. However, she did not teach them. Marjorie learned to fly at the Wright School in Dayton, Ohio, and received her license in August 1914.

During 1914, Stinson flew at county fairs. She tucked her long brown curls into a blue-and-white-checkered cap, leaving one curl to hang over her shoulder. Because of her youthful appearance, she became known as "The Flying Schoolgirl," although she was twenty-three years old at the time. Crowds gasped at the aerial stunts this tiny, fearless woman performed. "Fear, as I understand it," Stinson said, "is simply due to a lack of confidence or to lack of knowledge—which is the same thing. If I think my machine is all right and know that I can manage it, I am not afraid."

In 1915, she added more stunts to her repertoire. On

Katherine Stinson, dubbed "The Flying Schoolgirl," stands next to the wooden propeller of her plane. (Smithsonian Institution)

July 18, in Chicago, Illinois, she first flew a loop-the-loop. Few male pilots at the time attempted this dangerous feat because the plane could stall at the top of the loop and would crash unless the pilot could restart the plane. Stinson made sure she gained enough altitude so that if the engine did quit, she would have time to start it again before she hit the ground. She did another loop-the-loop in August and added a new twist. At the top of the loop, she made a snap roll by rolling her plane, wing over wing.

On December 17, 1915, in Los Angeles, Stinson became the first pilot to do skywriting. She attached magnesium flares to her wings and traced "CAL" (for California) in the night sky. The lights and smoke momentarily blinded her, but she managed to land her plane.

At the beginning of 1916, the Stinsons moved to San Antonio, Texas, where Katherine organized the Stinson School of Flying. Her mother continued as business manager, while her sister taught most of the flight lessons. Marjorie trained Canadian cadets from 1914-1917; she became known as "The Flying Schoolmarm." Eddie graduated in 1916 and would later become a famous plane designer. Jack would run his own flying field in New York.

In May 1916, Stinson gave a spectacular performance at Sheepshead Bay Speedway on Long Island, New York. In addition to her aerial stunts that day, she raced an automobile and won. For added measure, she dropped eight cylinders of dynamite from her plane onto a skeletal fort. A month later, Stinson made an exhibition tour of Canada. One of her proudest moments came in Manitoba when the Sioux made her an honorary member of their tribe.

Toward the end of 1916, Stinson and her manager planned her most ambitious tour to date. She scheduled exhibition flights in Japan and China, beginning in December 1916 and continuing through the first five months of 1917.

As a mark of her growing fame, Stinson's trip to Japan was mentioned in *Billboard* magazine. Her manager, her mechanic, her mother, and a friend accompanied her on

Audiences across Asia adored Stinson's daring stunts. Here, hundreds of fans look on as Stinson takes off from Aoyama Parade Ground in Tokyo, Japan. (Library of Congress)

the trip. Stinson brought three planes with her on the ship. When traveling long distances, pilots would take their planes apart for shipment and then reassemble them at their destinations.

Stinson and her entourage headed first for Tokyo, where she planned a night flight over the city on December 16. One Tokyo newspaper estimated that 50,000 people gathered to see her perform. The spectators included Japanese army aviators who wanted to duplicate her aerial acrobatics. A military escort accompanied her to the parade grounds. Six hundred policemen lined the area, each holding a round paper lantern.

The aviator attached magnesium flares to the edges of her lower wings and climbed to about 1,500 feet. With flares outlining her maneuvers, she wrote a giant "S." The crowd went wild. When the plane wheels touched the ground, people rushed forward, wanting to see this daring woman pilot up close. The mob scene scared her more than anything she had ever experienced in the air.

She made thirty-five Japanese engagements, which included the cities of Yokohama, Nagasaki, Osaka, and Nagoya. Wherever she went, she created a sensation. The Japanese press followed her everywhere. When the crowds saw her, the people shouted, "Banzai," meaning, "[May you live] ten thousand years!"

Japanese women, considered second-class citizens in their country, were particularly taken with Katherine. They organized "Welcome Miss Stinson" clubs in Yokohama and Tokyo. Every day when she awoke, she had fifty to seventy-five fan letters waiting for her. Geishas in Osaka sent her flowers.

Katherine also inspired young people. They organized Stinson clubs across Japan. One schoolboy wrote:

How waiting we were that you come. I read your skillful arts and looping in the newspapers. And last night when I saw you that were flying high in the darkest sky I could not help to cry: you are indeed Air Queen! This word is not fair speech. Madam, I wish you health and happiness for purpose of airoplain [sic] society for a long, long time. Madam, please remember than I am Japanese student and wanting to make myself air-man if I can.

The Japanese showered her with gifts. The city of Tokyo and ten other organizations presented her with medals. The Japanese Women's club honored her with a $3,000 pearl necklace, and the Imperial Aero Club gave her a diamond ring with twelve stones. A woman in the Japanese royal family presented her with a $500 silk kimono, which she wore while flying—much to the delight of the crowds.

Stinson continued her Asian tour by flying in Peking, China. On March 11th, she gave an exhibition on the sacred ground of the Temple of Agriculture. City leaders attended, including the foreign minister. Thousands more watched from outside the temple. In the air, Stinson looped three times in quick succession. As she descended in a spiral, the right control stick snapped off in her hand. She had to bend over to grasp the stub to maintain control of her airplane. Stinson bobbed up and down to see over the dashboard while she maneuvered the broken control. She landed the plane with no further damage. Impressed, the president of China, Li Yung Hung, gave her a beautiful diamond pin.

She made thirty-two flights in China and was hugely popular. Before she left, the president presented her with more gifts: a personal check for thousands of dollars and a silver loving cup, which became one of her most cherished possessions. He called her, "Miss Shih Lien Sun, Granddaughter of Heaven."

In April 1917, the United States entered World War I, and Katherine Stinson returned to the United States because she thought her country needed her. She attempted twice to enlist as a combat pilot during the war, but the military refused to take her because she was a woman.

The Red Cross asked her to fly a fund-raising campaign for the war effort. In June 1917, she made a flight from Buffalo, New York, to Washington, DC, with stops in Syracuse, Albany, New York, and Philadelphia. Stinson flew a Curtiss JN "Jenny," the combat aircraft used by the U.S. Army in World War I. Stinson had never flown a Jenny before, so she practiced for fifteen minutes before she took off. Along the way, she dropped Red Cross leaflets and took pledges wherever she stopped. When she landed in Washington, she had collected pledges worth $2 million.

On December 11, 1917, flying a Curtiss biplane built to her specifications, Stinson made a nonstop flight

Stinson's fund-raising flights resulted in significant conributions during the Red Cross's War Fund drive. The Red Cross raised hundreds of millions of dollars for the war effort, as advertised in this 1917 archival poster. (Library of Congress)

from San Diego, California, to San Francisco. She had been most concerned about gaining enough altitude to cross the Tehachapi Mountains east of Los Angeles. She ran into strong head winds but cleared the peaks at 9,000 feet, higher than she had ever flown. She had carried her knitting with her but had no time to do it. Passing over Bakersfield, children waved to her and she returned the greeting, although she knew she was too high for them to see her wave. Stinson flew over the Golden Gate Bridge and landed at the Presidio in San Francisco. The aviator had started the trip with seventy-six gallons of gas. When she landed, she had two gallons left. But Stinson had set a long-distance nonstop record of 610 miles in nine hours and ten minutes, a new endurance record.

On May 23, 1918, Stinson set off to fly the U.S. mail from Chicago to New York City, the same route the pilot Ruth Law had flown a year and a half earlier. Over Binghamton, New York, she ran out of gas and had to land on a mountainside. However, she had made the 783-mile trip in ten hours, ten minutes, another new endurance record. She said she felt certain Ruth Law would have been pleased to know that her record had been broken by another woman. Two months later, on July 9, Katherine Stinson became the first civilian to carry airmail for the Canadian government.

Stinson still wanted to be more directly involved in the war effort, so she went to France to work as an ambulance driver for the Red Cross. The long hours and stressful conditions affected her health. She contracted influenza and returned to the United States. When her illness turned into tuberculosis, she moved to the high, dry climate of Santa Fe, New Mexico, to recover. In 1920, at the age of twenty-nine, Katherine Stinson retired from flying.

In 1928, she married Judge Miguel Otero Jr., a former World War I pilot. She studied architecture and became a designer of houses, winning several awards. But her health still suffered, and by 1962 she was bedridden. Katherine Stinson died July 8, 1977 in Santa Fe, at the age of eighty-six.

The fearless Flying Schoolgirl once told a reporter, "It seems to me so simple to say, 'Well, if other people have done this I don't see why I can't.'" And so she did.

TIMELINE

1891	Born in Fort Payne, Alabama, on February 14.
1912	Makes first solo flight; receives pilot's license; becomes fourth woman to earn pilot's license in U.S.
1913	Gives first exhibition flight; becomes first woman to carry U.S. airmail.
1915	Performs her first loop-the-loop; becomes first pilot to perform night skywriting.
1916	Begins exhibition flights in Japan and China.
1917	Raises funds for the American Red Cross by flying; sets nonstop distance and endurance record.
1918	Sets endurance record; becomes first civilian to fly airmail for Canadian government; drives an ambulance for Red Cross in France.
1977	Dies in Santa Fe, New Mexico, on July 8.

Ruth Law. (Library of Congress)

Ruth Law

QUEEN OF THE AIR

"No woman will ever be able to fly!" said Wilbur Wright to Ruth Law when she asked to take flying lessons in 1912. But she didn't let this remark stop her. If anyone told Ruth she couldn't do something, she set out to prove she could.

Nothing in Ruth Law's youth indicated she would become a famous aviator. She was born on March 21, 1887, in Lynn, Massachusetts. Her father, a former naval officer, and her mother ensured she had a proper education at Miss Livermore's finishing school. Ruth's older brother Rodman was one of the first men in the United States to do parachute jumps, earning the nickname "The Human Fly." He also performed aerial stunts for motion pictures. Rodman inspired his sister to take to the air and proved to be the greatest influence in her life.

In 1907, Ruth Law married Charles Oliver, who raced automobiles. She retained her maiden name for professional reasons. Oliver also had an interest in aviation but was too nervous to pilot an airplane. He knew his wife wanted to fly, so he encouraged her to buy a plane. Ruth Law picked out a thirty-five horsepower Wright Model B biplane and ordered it shipped to Lynn, Massachusetts. Orville Wright doubted she could fly the plane, but he sold it to her anyway.

Law took her first ride on July 1, 1912, at the Boston Air Meet, the same day she watched Harriet Quimby fall to her death. Though shaken, Law would not be deterred. Four days later, she took her first flight lesson and made her first solo flight on August 1, 1912. In October, the eager pilot flew at the Columbus Day Meet on Staten Island, New York, where she created a sensation. On November 12, 1912, Ruth Law received her pilot's license (#188) from the Aero Club.

For her aerial performances, she designed and sewed her own black satin flying suit, which included knicker pants, a black cap pulled over her blonde hair, and knee-high black leather boots. Ruth Law's husband became her business manager.

A resort hotel in Sea Breeze, Florida, offered Law a contract to carry its guests on plane rides. During the winter months of 1913-1914, Law made daily flights at the resort, charging wealthy passengers up to $50 each. It was in Florida where she gave a performance that earned her a place in baseball lore.

Young Ruth Law at the controls of her plane shortly after earning her pilot's license. (Library of Congress)

Wilbert "Uncle Robbie" Robinson, manager of the Brooklyn Dodgers, asked Law to throw him the first pitch in an exhibition game. She had to throw the ball from her plane at an altitude higher than the Washington Monument. As Law readied for her flight, she realized she did not have a baseball. A mechanic did have a grapefruit in his lunch box. That would have to do. Soaring above the baseball diamond, Law flung the grapefruit. It hit Uncle Robbie smack in the chest, knocking him on his back. As the grapefruit juice oozed into his uniform, Uncle Robbie yelled for help, thinking he was bleeding to death. Law looked on in horror while the crowd roared.

During the summer months of 1913, Law toured in the eastern United States. In July, she gave a night performance, flying with electric lights on her plane. She made tours of the Midwest that fall, sometimes teaming with aviator Katherine Stinson, a friend and competitor. Unlike most touring fliers who shipped their aircraft by rail, Law put her plane on a flatbed truck and pulled it behind her automobile. She not only saved railroad express charges, but she was sure to have her plane at the next exhibition on time.

In August 1914, with her parents watching, she flew with her brother Rodman, who parachuted from the plane to land on a marked spot on the ground. Their mother never understood how she could have children who did such dangerous things. Stunt work, even though it lasted no more than twenty minutes, was intense and challenging. Law did fancy needlework between shows to help her relax.

Law is photographed with her mother and a group of admiring men after completing a flight. (Library of Congress)

In 1915, Law bought a Curtiss one hundred-horse-power biplane from aircraft designer Glenn Curtiss, one of many men who thought women had no business flying. On January 17, 1915, she did a loop-the-loop with the plane. The April 24, 1915 issue of *Billboard,* a daily publication that featured entertainment news, carried an ad proclaiming that in an upcoming exhibition, "The Queen of the Air" would do the "Dip of Death" and "Steep Banking" in addition to her famous loop-the-loop.

Ruth Law's husband said of his wife, "She's an instinctive flier. She anticipates what's coming before it happens. She doesn't wait until the wind strikes her and then push her levers [plane controls]. She pushes them first and is ready to meet that wind." However, he became so nervous when she flew that he hid in the hanger and came out only when someone told him she had come down safely.

In May 1916, on Sheepshead Bay, New York, Law competed against male pilots to set an altitude record. Again her parents watched from the stands. The plane's barograph, which measured the height of her ascent, recorded her altitude at 11,200 feet. Ruth Law had set a new altitude record for women, but she came in second overall. Even though she won $250, she was upset she did not beat the first-place winner.

Ruth Law's greatest aviation achievement came in November 1916. She decided to attempt a nonstop long-distance record by flying from Chicago, Illinois, to New York City, a distance of almost nine hundred miles—despite the fact she had never flown farther than twenty-five miles at any one time. Two weeks earlier, pilot Victor Carlstrom had attempted this same route but was forced down at Erie, Pennsylvania, because of a broken fuel line.

On the morning of November 19, Law arose in Chicago early and dressed for her flight. She donned two wool flying suits and two leather suits, then pulled high leather boots over her shoes. A wool face mask and a helmet of leather and wool went over her head. Long leather gloves completed her flying outfit.

Law, in her snug flying outfit, on the runway in Chicago before departing on her historic flight to New York. (Library of Congress)

After Law and her husband arrived at Grant Park on the shore of Lake Michigan, she did a thorough check of her Curtiss biplane. For this flight, she had made several innovative modifications to the boxy little aircraft. Originally, it had held only eight gallons of gas, but she added auxiliary tanks that brought the fuel capacity up to fifty-three gallons. Law also installed a rubber fuel line, which was less likely to break than metal.

To keep her maps from blowing out of the open cockpit, she designed a special map case with a glass top. She cut strips of survey maps and glued them to a piece of fabric attached to rollers. The scrolled map fit inside the metal case, which Law strapped to her left leg. Beforehand, she marked her route and her compass directions on the map. As backup, she also wrote a summary of the compass directions on the cuff of her right glove.

A handful of people gathered to watch her takeoff, including an official of the Aero Club of America. At first the plane would not start because of the cold.

A newspaper reporter snaps a photograph of Law shortly after her takeoff from Chicago's Grant Park on the morning of November 19, 1916. (Library of Congress)

Finally, the mechanics started the engine, and Law stepped aboard. The pilot's seat (often called the "undertaker's seat" because so many early aviators lost their lives while flying) rested on the lower wing, in front of the engine. Looking like a big bundle of wool and leather, Law sat with her hands on the two controls. Only her blue eyes showed through her goggles.

Law lifted off at 7:30 AM, Central Standard Time. The plane climbed sluggishly, buffeted by winds coming off Lake Michigan. She turned and headed east. Checking her map, Law noted her next city: Gary, Indiana. Because she could not let go of the left vertical control, she turned the knobs on the map case with her right hand, using her knee for a moment to keep the right control steady.

The flight went well until the plane ran out of gas as Law approached Hornell, New York. She glided down to a landing. Ruth looked at her clock, which read 2:10 PM. She had flown 590 miles in five hours and forty-five minutes. She had broken Victor Carlstrom's nonstop distance record by 138 miles. Not only had she set a United States distance record, she had also flown the second fastest nonstop trip in the world (the first was made by a Frenchman).

After lunch, she refueled and set off for Binghamton, New York, nearly ninety miles away. She flew about one hundred miles an hour. At 4:20, she landed at the Binghamton racetrack. Law considered continuing on to New York and her final destination, Governors Island, site of a U.S. Army base, but darkness had settled in, and so she spent the night.

Shortly after takeoff from Binghamton the next morning, she ran into thick fog and could not see any landmarks. Her compass and maps proved useless to her now. Law descended and flew close to the ground. She dipped over valleys and climbed when she saw hills. Fortunately, she was accustomed to flying near the ground when she raced automobiles.

Finally, she spotted the Susquehanna River and followed it until it turned south. The flier headed east and flew over the Delaware River. When Law reached the Hudson River, she followed it down to New York City. Cold and dampness now penetrated her four layers of clothing. Her hands felt frozen to the controls.

Over Upper Manhattan, her engine started to sputter. She knew the plane had little fuel left. Opposite 23rd Street, her motor cut out. She banked the plane, which allowed the remaining gas to reach the carburetors. She flew upwards, trying to gain altitude for her descent. The plane had no more fuel—it floated on a current of air. Finally, Law saw Governors Island at the mouth of the East River. The aviator made a long graceful turn and glided downward—"A hundred and twenty pounds of pluck," *Flyer* magazine called her afterwards.

Ruth Law landed at 9:37:35 AM. She had flown 884 miles in eight hours, fifty-five minutes, and thirty-five seconds. An Army brass band played, and a garrison of soldiers stood at attention. The many well-wishers present included Victor Carlstrom, gracious in defeat. Ruth said later of her achievement, "My flight was done with no

A small crowd accompanies Law in her airplane shortly after her victorious arrival at Governors Island, New York. (Library of Congress)

expectation of reward, just purely for the love of accomplishment."

But the rewards came. In December, Law was honored at dinner in a New York hotel with President and Mrs. Woodrow Wilson in attendance. Later that month, the Aero Club hosted a dinner for her where she sat between Admiral Robert Peary, discoverer of the North Pole, and Roald Amundsen, the first man to reach the South Pole. The aviator received $2,500 and heard many congratulatory speeches.

Ruth Law made another thriller flight that month. On December 2, New York City celebrated the installation of electric floodlights illuminating the Statue of Liberty. Up to that time, the statue had electric lights only in the torch. (In February 1912, Rodman Law had parachuted from Liberty's torch.) The French ambassador and the United States president attended, as did many other dignitaries. President Wilson, from his presidential yacht, gave the signal to turn on the floodlights. Looking like a giant sparkler, Ruth Law flew over the Statue of Liberty with magnesium flares blazing from her wings. The underside of her plane carried an electric sign that spelled out "Liberty."

But not all the news was good. World War I had begun two years before and was devastating Europe. Though Wilson had won reelection based on his opposition to U.S. involvement in the war, it seemed inevitable American troops would be needed. World War I marked the first use of airplanes in combat. A New York newspaper asked Law to report on this development in aviation. In January 1917, she and her husband sailed to Europe to tour airplane factories and training fields in France and Britain. A French aircraft designer took her up in his new plane and flew an astounding 198 miles per hour over Paris. She was more fascinated with the plane than with seeing the Eiffel Tower.

On April 6, 1917, the United States entered the war. Law returned home and petitioned the U.S. War Department to let her fly combat missions in Europe. The military refused her offer but said she could help in other ways. The U.S. Army did send her a noncommissioned officer's uniform, which she wore while doing recruiting tours.

She also flew fund-raising benefits for the Red Cross and sold Liberty Bonds to raise money for the war effort. One of her most memorable flights occurred in Washington, DC, when she flew down Pennsylvania Avenue, which runs from the White House to the Capitol. She skimmed thirty feet above the street, going ninety miles an hour. The city had never seen anything like it.

Law most liked racing her plane against automobiles, the most dangerous of stunts, since she flew only about twenty-five feet above the ground. She once told a reporter, "The real aviator lacks nerves. What is called bravery is simply a lack of nerves."

For a year and a half she gave up her exhibition career, which earned her up to $9,000 weekly, and flew all over the country, recruiting soldiers and raising money. How-

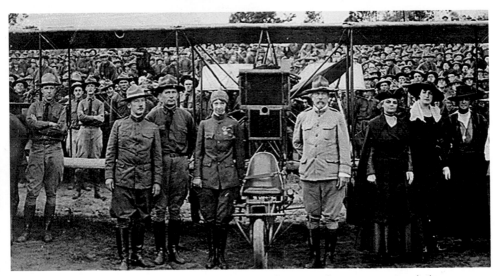

Law, the only woman of her time permitted to wear the government aviation uniform for nonmilitary purposes, stands with members of the 29th Division at Camp McClellan, Alabama, during World War I. (National Archives)

ever, she could not resist making another competitive flight. In September 28, 1917, she set a new women's altitude record of 14,700 feet in Peoria, Illinois.

After the war ended in November 1918, Law returned to her lucrative flying career. She and her husband started Ruth Law's Flying Circus, which included two male pilots and three planes. In one stunt, she climbed out of her plane and walked out to the middle of the aircraft while the pilot went through three consecutive loops. A heart-stopping performance—but a carefully calculated one. She knew the centrifugal force would pin her flat against the plane.

In 1919, Law and her husband toured China, Japan, and the Philippines. On April 5, she became the first woman to deliver mail in the Philippines. By this time, Ruth Law had become wealthy, but she continued to perform because she liked the thrill of flying and enjoyed the contact with famous people.

While Law did ever more dangerous stunts, Charles Oliver grew increasingly troubled about his wife's flying. One day in 1922, she picked up the morning newspaper and read that she had retired from flying. Her husband had placed the story. Because she feared for his health, Ruth Law quit flying. She also knew the odds of being killed while doing a stunt.

Ruth Law retired to Beverly Hills, California, where she tended her rock garden and did woodcarving. She later told a reporter, "I don't care what Wilbur Wright said, I think every woman should learn to fly—it's good for them. Only, they will have to train their husbands not to have nervous breakdowns."

Ruth Law never lost her interest in aviation. She studied the early helicopter and declared it the aircraft of the future. She even considered making a solo flight across the Atlantic Ocean, but in 1927, Charles Lindbergh became the first pilot to accomplish this feat. In 1946, Law told a reporter that she fully expected there would be a flight to the moon someday.

Years after her husband died in 1947, Ruth Law took a ride in a friend's private plane. He asked if she would like to take over the controls—and she did. Twenty-five years after she gave up flying, the former Queen of the Air, now seventy-one-years old, flew once more.

Ruth Law died on December 3, 1970, at the age of eighty-three. She was buried in Lynn, Massachusetts.

TIMELINE

1887	Born in Lynn, Massachusetts, on March 21.
1912	Takes first flight lesson in July; receives her pilot's license (#188) in November.
1913	Makes a moonlight flight over Staten Island, New York.
1915	Flies her first loop-the-loop.
1916	Sets an aviation distance record, flying from Chicago, Illinois, to New York City in eight hours, fifty-five minutes; becomes first woman to fly over the Statue of Liberty.
1917-1918	Performs exhibition flights to recruit for U.S. Army; does fund-raising for the Red Cross; sells Liberty Bonds; sets women's altitude record of 14,700 feet; organizes Ruth Law's Flying Circus.
1919	Becomes first woman to carry airmail in Philippines.
1922	Retires from flying.
1970	Dies on December 3; buried in Lynn, Massachusetts.

Bessie Coleman. (Smithsonian Institution)

Bessie Coleman
BLACK JOAN OF ARC

At her birth, Bessie Coleman had three things working against her: she was poor, she was black, and she was a female. However, she possessed a keen mind, an eagerness to learn, and determination—great determination. This first African-American woman aviator set out to prove she would "amount to something."

Bessie was born January 26, 1892, in Atlanta, Texas, a small farming community in northeast Texas about ten miles from the Arkansas border. When Bessie was two, her family moved to Waxahachie, about thirty miles south of Dallas. Her parents, Susan and George Coleman, bought a quarter acre of land and built a three-room house on an unpaved road outside town.

As a child, Bessie watered the many flowers growing

in the front yard. She also helped her mother with the vegetable garden and orchard in the back. When Bessie turned nine, her father, who was part Choctaw, left for Indian Territory in Oklahoma, where he would have more rights as a citizen. Bessie's mother refused to go. To support her children, Susan Coleman worked as a maid in a white household. Bessie's three older brothers left home to find work in the North, so she had the care of her three younger sisters. She cleaned, washed, and ironed, all without running water or electricity in the house.

Her mother was the most important influence in Bessie's early life. Although Susan Coleman could not read or write, she wanted her children to be educated— to amount to something, she said. Bessie read books that her mother checked out from a traveling library wagon. The child was always reading, always learning. She often woke her sister Elois at two or three in the morning so they could "think." Bessie would introduce a subject and expect Elois to respond. She told Elois that people did not spend enough time thinking.

Religion played an important part in the life of the Coleman family. Every evening, Bessie read Bible verses aloud. On Sundays, the family attended the Missionary Baptist church. Sitting in the pew, Bessie heard sermons on how God created everyone equal. She helped with a church fund-raiser and won a hand organ for selling the most raffle tickets.

In spring and summer, Bessie earned money by helping her mother wash and iron other people's clothes. During the fall, she helped pick cotton, a job she hated. She lagged behind and sometimes rode on others' cotton sacks as they picked. Bessie kept the family's records of how much cotton they picked and the money they earned. If the foreman was not looking, she put her foot on the scales to increase the weight of the cotton.

With cotton season over, Bessie attended the segregated school in Waxahachie. She walked four miles to her one-room school, which often had no textbooks or even pencil and paper. She loved school and excelled in math, even though she had to miss many days because she had to care for her sisters.

When Bessie finished her schooling at the end of the eighth grade, she wanted to attend college. However, she

Cotton was one of the only industries in Waxahachie when Bessie Coleman was growing up there. This photograph shows a family, including young children, at work in the Waxahachie cotton fields in the early 1900s. (Library of Congress)

had no money, so she took in washing and ironing. With her small savings, she attended the Colored Agricultural and Normal University in Langston, Oklahoma. But her money ran out after one term. She brought the college band to accompany her to the homecoming her church held for her.

Bessie Coleman had no intention of staying in Waxahachie, where she would have been limited to cleaning houses, washing and ironing, or working in the cotton fields. She wanted to make something of herself, so in 1915 she headed north to Chicago to join her two older brothers. Within three years, her mother and her sisters and their children followed her to Chicago.

Coleman took a manicure course and found a job doing nails in a barbershop on black Chicago's main street. In January 1916, she obtained a marriage license to marry Claude Glenn, a quiet older man. Her family did not know about the marriage until years later. They lived apart but saw each other from time to time.

In April 1917, the United States entered World War I. (Bessie's two older brothers served in France.) For the first time, the U.S. Army used planes in combat. Coleman became interested in the aircraft she read about in the newspapers. One day a small boy brought a toy plane into the barbershop, which so delighted Coleman that she hung the plane in the window. She decided to become an aviator when her brother John teased her about American black women not being able to fly. She smiled and said, "You just called it for me."

Coleman applied to flight schools in the United States, but they refused to accept her because she was black and because she was a woman. When she told Robert Abbott, publisher of the *Chicago Defender* newspaper, that she wanted to fly, he suggested she go to France for flight instruction. She took French lessons while she managed a chili parlor. She worked long hard hours trying to save enough money to go to France. Her family thought flying was too dangerous and objected to her plans, but Coleman was determined. Her mother later laughed and said, "I had thirteen kids, raised nine, and one's crazy."

When Coleman arrived in France in 1920, she had difficulty finding a flight school that would accept her—not because of her skin color, but because she was a woman. Finally she found a school in Le Crotoy, the place where Joan of Arc, teenage leader of the French army, had been imprisoned by the English in 1430. Coleman studied in Le Crotoy for seven months, walking nine miles each day to her lessons. She earned her flying certificate on June 15, 1921, six months before Amelia Earhart received her pilot's license. Coleman was twenty-nine years old, although she gave her age as twenty-five.

In February 22, 1922, Bessie returned to the United States. Black newspapers across the country carried accounts of this first African-American woman aviator, and she received enormous attention from the black population. In New York, she was the guest of honor at the play "Shuffle Along." The black cast gave her a silver

Bessie Coleman stands next to a Nieuport, the type of plane she learned to fly in France.

cup, and the audience—black and white—rose to applaud her.

Aware that she needed more flight instruction, Coleman went back to France where German and French war aviators taught her aerobatics. She performed in Paris and Amsterdam, piloting a Fokker plane, a combat aircraft used by the Germans during World War I. In Berlin, she made more than fifty flights, and she appeared in films for the German Pathe News. During one performance, she flew over the kaiser's (the German ruler's) palace.

In August 1922, Coleman returned to the United States, ready to show off her new flying skills. Using a borrowed Curtiss plane, she made her first solo flight on

Air shows were a popular form of entertainment in France, and the craze quickly spread to the United States in the early part of the century. (Musée de l'air, Paris)

September 3 over Curtiss Field on Long Island, New York. She did not do any aerobatics because owner Glenn Curtiss did not allow stunt flying in his planes. She next appeared October 12 in Memphis, Tennessee, becoming the first black woman to fly in the South.

Coleman looked forward to her exhibition flight in

her adopted hometown of Chicago. On October 15, 1922, she gave a dazzling performance in a borrowed plane at the Checkerboard Airdome. Two thousand people attended, including her proud mother, her sisters, nieces, and one nephew. The black community went ecstatic over Bessie Coleman. The *Chicago Defender* dubbed her "Queen Bess." When a reporter asked why she wanted to fly, she said, "We must have aviators if we are to keep up with the times. I shall never be satisfied until we have men of the [black] Race who can fly. Do you know you have never lived until you have flown?"

This "Black Joan of Arc," as she billed herself, had made up her mind to open a school of aviation for African Americans. She earned money by lecturing, offering exhibition rides, and performing aerial stunts. Sometimes she drew up to 10,000 spectators for her shows. In Boston, she flew loops over the spot where her hero, Harriet Quimby, had plunged to her death.

Not all went well for Coleman. After she performed in Chicago, she signed a contract to make a movie. When she learned she would be playing an illiterate girl, she refused to be a part of the movie. Over the next few years, she worked with several different managers and agents, developing a reputation as being difficult to work with.

By 1923, Coleman had made enough money to buy her own plane, a used Curtiss JN-4 "Jenny." She found a sponsor in Coast Tire and Rubber Company in Oakland, California. In return for expenses paid, Coleman dropped advertising leaflets for the company.

On February 4, 1923, Coleman suffered a serious accident in Santa Monica, California, when her Jenny stalled and crashed. She broke three ribs and her leg in several places and spent three months in the hospital. She said, "You tell the world I'm coming back." When her sister Elois remarked that the accident would be the end of Coleman's flying career, her mother said, "Oh, you don't know Bess."

She went back to Chicago and rested for eighteen months. There she spent time with her family. Coleman never had children of her own and doted on her nieces and nephews. She cooked for them, gave them attention, bought toys and clothes, and gave them spending money.

In May 1925, Coleman arrived in Houston, Texas, where she set up a base of operations for her planned barnstorming appearances in that state. In addition to stunting, she made dangerous parachute jumps and participated in air races. In June 1925, she gave shows in Houston, Galveston, San Antonio, and Austin. (Coleman told her sister Elois that the Texas governor, Miriam A. "Ma" Ferguson, entertained her at the governor's mansion there.) She also performed in smaller Texas towns, and in September, she put Waxahachie on her itinerary.

It had been more than ten years since thirty-three-year-old Coleman had left the place of her childhood. Amid great acclaim from the African-American community, Coleman arrived in Waxahachie on Tuesday, September 22, 1925. The white-owned newspaper,

Waxahachie Daily Light, published an article about her homecoming, noting that she would give a performance at the sports grounds at Trinity University. In an interview for the article, Coleman extended an invitation to the mayor of Waxahachie, officials of Trinity University, and the editorial staff of the paper to fly as her passengers.

In the days before her aerobatic show, Coleman most likely gave talks to black churches, clubs, and schools. When she lectured, she often showed moving pictures of her flights over the kaiser's palace. She wanted to reach two audiences: black women—who were more receptive than men to her career—and black youth, whom she wanted to interest in aviation. She felt that the sky was the only place where African Americans could be free.

The headlines of September 25th edition of the *Waxahachie Daily Light* read "Bessie Coleman, Negro, to Fly Here Saturday." The newspaper featured a large picture of a smiling Coleman standing in front of her plane. She was dressed in a stylish flying uniform tailored in France: an olive-colored, belted tunic and riding breeches, a matching cap, and high-laced boots.

On Saturday afternoon, September 26, 1925, a large crowd gathered at the university athletic field. University officials had planned two admission entrances, one for whites and one for blacks. Coleman informed them that she would not perform under this arrangement. They compromised: there would be one admission gate, but segregated seating within. Coleman did not like the situation, but she agreed to it.

Coleman in one of her flight uniforms in the early 1920s. (Library of Congress)

Coleman followed a certain ritual before each of her performances. She would enter the roped-off area where the plane took off and landed. Wearing her uniform and a long leather coat, Coleman kept her flying goggles up so the audience could see her face. After listening to a prayer said for her safety, she walked to her plane and posed for pictures. Finally, she pulled down her goggles, climbed into the cockpit, and took off. Her figure eights, barrel rolls, loop-the-loops, stalls, dives, and glides brought gasps and shrieks from the spectators below. It was a very successful homecoming.

During one of her tours, her plane stalled in midair. Coleman managed to restart the plane but still cut her performance short and headed toward the ground. Her manager knew something was wrong and rushed to the landing site. Coleman landed the plane safely, got out, and waved to the cheering crowd.

A small boy sneaked under the ropes and walked toward the pilot. Amused, she beckoned him to continue forward. Once he reached her, he looked back to see if he was being chased. He said, "Lady, didn't your plane stop up there for awhile?"

The aviator was astonished this young child could be so observant. Yes, she admitted, the plane had stalled. She laughed and took him into her arms and hugged him. With a smug look on his face, he turned and strutted back to the still-cheering crowd.

Coleman found she could earn a steady income as a lecturer, so she planned speaking tours across the South. She had two goals: to earn enough money to open her aviation school and to finish paying for a used plane she had found in Dallas. The aviator gave her first lecture in Savannah, Georgia, the first week in January 1926. Then she moved on to Tampa and West Palm Beach, Florida. In Orlando, Florida, she stayed with a black minister and his wife until the end of February.

After a few months, Coleman had enough money to make the final payment on the plane. Her mechanic/manager flew the aircraft from Dallas to Jacksonville, Florida, experiencing many breakdowns and delays on the way. Coleman planned an exhibition flight on May 1, 1926, before a Jacksonville crowd.

The day before her scheduled appearance, she decided to do a practice parachute jump. Normally a cautious aviator, she did not buckle her safety belt that day. With her mechanic at the controls, the plane spun out of control at 3,500 feet and plunged toward the earth. It flipped over at five hundred feet, and Bessie fell out. She and her mechanic both died in the crash. An investigation discovered that a loose wrench had jammed the plane's control gears.

Rescuers found a note in the pocket of Bessie Coleman's uniform. In it, Ruby Mae McDuffie, a twelve-year-old, wrote, "I am writing you to congratulate you on your brave doings. I want to be an aviatrix when I get [to be] a woman. I like to see our own Race do brave things. I am going to be out there to see you jump from the airplane. I want an airplane of my own when I get [to be] a woman."

The aviator had two funerals, one in Orlando and another in Chicago. Over two days, 10,000 people filed past her casket. No one could doubt that Bessie Coleman had amounted to something.

TIMELINE

1892	Born in Atlanta, Texas, on January 26.
1915	Moves to Chicago, Illinois.
1920	Goes to France to take flying lessons; becomes first black woman to fly a plane.
1921	Earns pilot's license, issued by the Federation Aeronautique Internationale (FAI).
1922	Makes solo flight; becomes the first black woman to pilot a plane in U.S.
1923	Crashes plane in Santa Monica, California.
1925	Makes exhibition flight in Waxahachie, Texas.
1926	Dies in plane crash on April 30.
1995	Honored by U.S. Postal Service stamp.

Amelia Earhart. (Library of Congress)

Amelia Earhart

AVIATION ADVOCATE

Amelia Earhart flew for the fun of it, she always said. But this most famous of women aviators used her name and achievements to promote causes that mattered to her. She wanted to prove that flying was safe and that women made good pilots. A. E., as she called herself, advanced these beliefs through her writings and her many speeches—and through her well-publicized flights.

Amelia Earhart was born July 24, 1897, in Atchison, Kansas, to Amy and Edwin Earhart. Her father traveled as a lawyer for a railroad, so Amelia and her sister Muriel lived with their maternal grandmother. Growing up, Amelia liked sports such as basketball, tennis, and riding horses. She read constantly. "Books meant much to me," she said.

Until 1912, Amelia and her sister lived in this house with their grandmother in Atchison, Kansas, on a high bluff overlooking the Missouri River. (National Archives)

After their grandmother died in 1912, the girls went to live with their parents. Amelia went to six different high schools in four years and particularly enjoyed chemistry and physics. In 1916, she graduated from Hyde Park High School in Chicago, Illinois. A classmate wrote in her yearbook, "A. E.—the girl in brown who walks alone."

Amelia Earhart spent her young adulthood searching for what she wanted to do with her life. After graduation, she went to a college preparatory school near Philadelphia. By 1917, she had dropped out to work as a nurse's aide at a military hospital in Toronto, Canada. She thought she might be interested in medicine, so in 1919, she enrolled at Columbia University in pre-medical studies. Earhart also became a photographer's assistant. "I've had twenty-eight different jobs in my life," she later said, "and I hope I'll have two hundred and twenty-eight more. Experiment! Meet new people! . . . You will find the unexpected."

Although Earhart saw her first plane at a county fair when she was ten, she did not become interested in flying until 1918, while watching stunt pilots in Canada. During the summer of 1919, she visited her family in California and attended air meets. Finally, in 1920, she asked a barnstormer to take her up. She said, "As soon as we left the ground, I knew I had to fly by myself. Miles away I saw the ocean . . . the Hollywood hills smiled at me over the edge of the cockpit. . . .We were friends, the ocean, the hills, and I." She had finally found what she wanted to do.

In Los Angeles in 1921, Earhart took flying lessons from Anita "Neta" Snooks, one of the earliest women flight instructors. Although Earhart worked diligently at her lessons, Snooks worried about her student's rough landings. On December 15, 1921, Earhart received her pilot's license. Her mother helped her pay for a used plane. When Snooks retired from flying in 1922, she turned her student over to John Montijo, a Mexican-American World War I pilot.

In 1926, Earhart moved to Boston to be near her sister and mother. (Her parents had divorced by this time.) She worked as a social worker at the Denison House, teaching English to immigrants. While she lived in Boston, a great aviation achievement occurred: on May 20, 1927, Charles Lindbergh flew his plane, *The Spirit of St. Louis,* across the Atlantic Ocean in thirty-three hours, thirty minutes. He became a great world hero and created enormous public interest in aviation.

Amy Guest, a wealthy American woman in England, wanted to see an American woman fly across the ocean. Guest asked George Palmer Putnam, who worked for the publishing company founded by his grandfather, to help her find the right person. He had heard about Earhart through friends of friends. In April 1928, Earhart received a phone call at work. Would she be interested in flying across the Atlantic Ocean as a passenger?

On June 17, 1928, Earhart left from Boston on the plane *Friendship* with pilot Wilmer Stultz and Louis Gordon, copilot and mechanic. They planned to fly from Newfoundland to the United Kingdom, the most direct route across the Atlantic. Earhart had the job of keeping the flight log and taking notes on the ride. After a flight of twenty hours and forty minutes, *Friendship* touched down at Burry Port, Wales, on June 18, 1928.

Earhart created almost as big a sensation as Charles Lindbergh had. Although she repeatedly said the two male pilots should receive the credit, it made little difference to the public—she became famous as the first woman to cross the Atlantic in a plane. For the next six months, she visited over thirty cities, made one hundred speeches, and gave two hundred interviews. When she appeared in public, people reached out to touch her skin, pat her hair, and tug at her clothes. The press dubbed her "Lady Lindy," a name she did not like. She bore a

After her flight across the Atlantic, Earhart became an instant American icon. Her image was used to sell a variety of products from cigarettes to luggage. This 1928 ad was part of a Lucky Strike campaign that featured celebrities including George Gershwin, Al Jolson, and Douglas Fairbanks Jr. (Library of Congress)

remarkable resemblance to Charles Lindbergh—tall and slender, with tousled sandy-colored hair.

Earhart wanted to pilot her own plane across the Atlantic, but she knew that she needed more flying experience. She had no interest in barnstorming, so she decided to enter competitive racing. On August 18, 1929, she became one of nineteen women pilots who competed in the first National Women's Air Derby, a race from Santa Monica, California, to Cleveland, Ohio. She came in third.

Earhart formed friendships with the other women in the race. From this core group came the Ninety-Nines, an organization of licensed women pilots. (Earhart suggested the name since there were ninety-nine charter members.) She became the organization's first president. Although she had many friends, none knew her well.

On February 11, 1931, Amelia Earhart married George Putnam at his mother's home in Connecticut. He made the arrangements for her many public appearances, handled her flight plans, and created the publicity for those flights. Family and friends thought her husband exerted too much control over her life, and many questioned his motives. But Earhart always remained very private about her marriage and about her personal life.

George Putnam also took care of his wife's busy speaking schedule. She often gave as many as twenty-

Earhart with her husband, George Putnam, on their wedding day in 1931. (Library of Congress)

seven speeches a month at $250 (about $2,600 in today's money) each. Earhart talked about the role of women in aviation and how safe it was to fly. She became an excellent speaker, a departure from her normally shy and reserved public persona. When she had time to come home to Rye, New York, she liked to garden. She also loved to dance.

In addition to lecturing, she accepted a position with *Cosmopolitan* magazine in 1928, writing about eight columns a year. She received as many as two hundred letters a day, many of them from young people. She answered most of her own mail. In addition to publishing three books, she also wrote poetry, most of it for her own pleasure. One poem, "Courage," became widely published: "Courage is the price Life exacts for granting peace / The soul who knows it not, knows no release / From little things." Unfortunately, a 1934 fire at her home destroyed most of her letters and poems.

Earhart became an advocate for commercial aviation, and in 1929 she worked as an assistant to the traffic manager of Transcontinental Air Transport. She gave many speeches about the safety of air travel, and to prove her point, she took her mother with her when she flew. In 1930, she helped establish the New York, Philadelphia, and Washington Airway, a shuttle service offering hourly flights between these cities. The aviator used her name and influence to interest passengers in the airline.

Earhart liked to experiment with the latest aviation

developments. She became interested in the autogiro, the forerunner of the helicopter. (Leonardo da Vinci first sketched this flying machine in 1483; Juan Cierva, a Spanish aeronautical engineer, designed the first successful autogiro in 1923.) The giro had the body of a plane with propellers that pulled it forward. An air-driven rotor, mounted on top, had four long, paddle-like blades. The hinged blades rose and fell with a feathering motion that lifted the giro up and down. After a ride, Earhart said about this difficult aircraft, "I am at a loss now to say whether I flew it or it flew me."

On April 8, 1931, Earhart set an autogiro altitude record by flying to 18,415 feet. She decided to fly the giro across the United States. She wanted to see how it would perform during a long trip under different kinds of conditions, and she also wanted to become the first person to fly one from coast to coast.

On May 29, 1931, Earhart and her mechanic left Newark, New Jersey, bound for Oakland, California. The giro cruised along at about eighty miles an hour. They made stops at numerous cities along the way. Alerted by George Putnam, local newspapers announced their arrivals, and huge crowds gathered to see the famous aviator flying this new aircraft. The press called it the "flying windmill" and the "paddle plane." At each stop, Earhart took a few people up for rides. After refueling, she lifted off for her next destination.

When she reached California on June 12, Earhart discovered that a male pilot had already made a transcontinental crossing in an autogiro the week before. Disappointed but undaunted, Earhart decided that if she could not be the first pilot to fly the giro from one coast to the other, then she would become the first person to make a round trip in the aircraft.

On the way home, Earhart crashed during liftoff in Abilene, Texas. She and her mechanic climbed out, unhurt. "While I regret any kind of accident," she later said, "I have found they are sometimes of benefit . . . I learned a great deal." The damaged giro was replaced, and they continued the trip. When the aviator arrived in Newark, New Jersey, on June 22, she had flown 11,000 miles in the aircraft. Amelia Earhart had greater achievements in aviation, but she took particular pride in testing the autogiro.

By May 1932, Earhart had accumulated 1,000 flying hours and completed instrument training. Now she felt ready to cross the Atlantic Ocean alone. Several other women had tried transatlantic flights, but each had failed. Earhart would fly a single-engine red-and-gold Lockheed Vega, which carried only absolute necessities, such as extra gasoline and oil.

During the evening of May 20, 1932, she lifted off from Harbor Grace, Newfoundland. She ran into a five-hour storm over the ocean. Ice formed on the wings, causing the plane to drop. When Earhart managed to pull up, she was low enough to see the foam on the waves. She also had another problem. When she looked back, she saw flames from the exhaust pipe. If the fire burned

This colorized photograph shows Earhart, surrounded by a crowd of fans, emerging from her plane after landing in rural Ireland. (Courtesy of the Granger Collection.)

through to the fuel line, the plane would explode. At dawn, the gas gauge on her reserve tanks ceased to work. Finally, she saw the coast of Ireland and set down near Londonderry, startling a farmer and his cows. She had flown across the Atlantic in fifteen hours and eighteen minutes.

But Earhart had not finished setting flying records. On August 24-25, 1932, she set a nonstop long-distance record flying from Los Angeles to Newark, New Jersey—2,447.728 miles in nineteen hours and five minutes. For her achievements, she received the 1932 Harmon Trophy for woman pilot of the year, the *National Geographic* gold medal, and the Distinguished Flying Cross from the U.S. Congress, becoming the first woman to achieve this honor.

As praise poured for her achievements, so did criticisms. Some aviators declared that she was careless and not a good pilot. Others said she sought publicity and that her flights were mere stunts. She replied, "To want in one's heart to do a thing for its own sake . . . isn't, I think, a reason to be apologized for by man or woman. It is the most honest motive for the majority of mankind's achievement."

Aviator Louise Thaden wrote about Amelia:

> A. E.'s personal ambitions were secondary to an insatiable desire to get women into the air; and once in the air to have the recognition she felt they deserved accorded them. I have known many women pilots she has helped either through financial assistance or moral encouragement. Further, she has talked more people into the air, most of them as passengers, others as pilots, than any other individual in aviation today.

And so Earhart continued to set records. On January 11, 1935, she flew from Mexico City to Newark, and set another record—2,125 miles in eighteen hours and eighteen minutes. She also became the first person to fly solo across the Pacific, going from Hawaii to San Francisco in January 1935.

That same year, Purdue University, in Indiana, appointed her as visiting professor of aviation. There, she gave lectures and lived in the girls' dorm. Students

Earhart with her Lockheed Electra, the plane she would attempt to fly around the world. (Library of Congress)

buzzed about having the famous aviator on campus. Talking to these young women about careers in aviation gave Earhart great satisfaction.

A university foundation bought her a Lockheed Electra, a twin-engine, ten-seater plane. Earhart wanted to test its reaction to high-altitude flight. She also intended to use the plane in her most ambitious project to date: a round-the-world flight, a distance of over 27,000 miles. Aviator friends tried to dissuade her from this trip. Too risky, they said, but Earhart would not listen.

On March 17, 1937, she set out on her west-to-east journey, starting from Oakland, California. In Honolulu, Hawaii, a tire blew out on the airport runway, and the Lockheed had to be shipped back to California for repairs. After waiting for two months, Earhart changed her plans and decided to fly from east to west because of weather conditions.

Earhart consults with her navigator, Fred Noonan, shortly before departing on their round-the-world flight in 1937. (Library of Congress)

Before she left on her final flight, she gave her husband a letter to be opened only if she did not return. On June 1, 1937, she took off from Miami, Florida, with her navigator Fred Noonan. This flight depended on radio communication, which would prove to be a major problem. Earhart was unfamiliar with the radio equipment onboard. Also, for unknown reasons, she did not take her trailing radio antenna, which meant she could not receive messages from long-distance radio operators based on land and sea.

Earhart spent the first six days of her flight going along the Central and South American coasts. Then she flew across the South Atlantic to Africa, India, and Southeast Asia. She left Lae, New Guinea, on July 2, heading for Howland Island, a tiny speck in the Pacific.

This 2,556-mile leg was the longest and most dangerous part of the journey.

Off Howland Island, the Coast Guard cutter *Itasca* waited for her communication. She established contact with the *Itasca* but did not stay on the radio long enough for the cutter to read her position in the sky. Because of the missing antenna, Earhart could not receive the messages the *Itasca* sent. At 9:00 PM, three hours after she was due to arrive, the Coast Guard put out a missing-plane alert to Washington, D.C. Search teams went out, which included 4,000 men, sixty-five planes, and nine ships. The search was finally called off on July 18.

Numerous rumors circulated about what happened to Amelia Earhart. Some people said she landed on an uninhabited island and starved to death. Others thought the aviator set down on an island occupied by Japanese soldiers who imprisoned her. A few speculated that the Japanese shot down her plane because she was on a secret mission for the United States government. Most aviation experts think that her plane simply ran out of fuel and sank into the ocean.

George Putnam opened Amelia's last letter. She had written, "I want to do it because I want to do it. Women must try to do things as men have tried. When they fail, their failure must be but a challenge to others."

TIMELINE

1897	Born in Atchison, Kansas, on July 24.
1921	Receives her private pilot's license.
1922	Sets altitude record of 14,000 feet.
1928	Becomes first woman to cross the Atlantic Ocean by air.
1930	Becomes first president of the Ninety-Nines.
1931	Becomes first woman to set autogiro altitude record at 18,415 feet; becomes first person to make a round-trip transcontinental flight in an autogiro.
1932	Becomes first woman to fly solo across the Atlantic Ocean; sets transcontinental distance record of 2,477.728 miles from Los Angeles to Newark, New Jersey, in nineteen hours, five minutes.
1935	First pilot to make solo flight across Pacific Ocean, from Hawaii to California; sets an international distance record, flying from Los Angeles, California, to Mexico City, in thirteen hours, thirty-three minutes; accepts an appointment as visiting professor at Purdue University in Lafayette, Indiana.
1937	Sets out from Miami, Florida, on June 1, to attempt a flight around the world; vanishes near Howland Island in the Pacific Ocean on July 2.

Ruth Nichols. (The Ninety-Nines, Oklahoma City)

Ruth Nichols

GRIT AND MERCY

*I*t is hard to imagine that Ruth Nichols had been a meek and fearful child. She set over thirty aviation records during the 1920s and 1930s. She survived six major plane crashes and always returned to the air. Few pilots—male or female—showed more sheer grit in the face of mortal danger than did Ruth Nichols. And none better used aviation to help people.

Ruth Rowland Nichols was born in New York City on February 23, 1901, to stockbroker Erickson Nichols (a direct descendant of Leif Erickson) and socialite Edith Hairies Nichols. Ruth, along with her sister and two younger brothers, had a privileged childhood. She grew up in a Manhattan brownstone and spent summers at lake homes or ocean resorts.

Ruth's father and maternal aunt influenced her most.

This image of Law with her Aunt Polly was taken in a photographer's studio in Atlantic City when Ruth was thirteen. (From Ruth Nichols' *Wings for Life*.)

Her father pushed his eldest child constantly. If she fell off a horse, she had to get back on. If she made a bad dive, she had to do it again. Ruth said, "It seemed as though I was forcing myself to tackle a terrifying job again and again." Her beloved Aunt Polly, a Quaker, proved to be a refuge from her father's pressures. "Aunty Angel," as Ruth called her, gave her gentle encouragement and support. She always turned to her aunt when she had problems or needed to make important decisions in her life.

As a graduation gift in 1919, Ruth's father gave her a ten-minute ride with Eddie Stinson, the World War I ace pilot. Scared stiff because she had a fear of heights, Ruth felt exhilarated when she landed. "My heart, however," she said, "remained in the sky."

Nichols enrolled at Wellesley College with the intention of becoming a physician. She made average grades but excelled in athletics, particularly riding and rowing crew. She also had several lead roles in plays. When she was a junior, she took off a year—at the request of her parents—to make her debut into society.

While wintering in Miami, Florida, Nichols paid for a fifteen-minute flight with Harry Rogers, barnstorming pilot of seaplanes. On the first ride, he let her take over the controls. She became enthralled with the beauty and freedom of flying. When Nichols returned home, she continued taking flight lessons from Rogers, who had moved his operations to New York. In 1924, she earned her license to fly hydroplanes, becoming the first woman in the United States to do so.

When Nichols graduated from Wellesley that same year, her parents sent her on a trip around the world. She flew as a passenger in a Navy bomber in Hawaii, drove a locomotive in India, and took a transport plane from France to England. Small wonder that when she returned to work in a bank, she grew bored and restless. She knew she belonged in the air.

By 1927, Ruth Nichols had earned her license to fly transport planes. That year, she was captivated by Charles Lindbergh's flight across the Atlantic. Nichols intended to become the first woman to make a solo transatlantic flight. Not only would she make a name for herself, she could earn money to help her father, who had suffered financial losses. She hired a technical aviation advisor to help her prepare for the perilous journey.

In January 1928, Harry Rogers asked her to be his co-pilot on a trip from New York City to Miami, Florida. It would be the first nonstop flight by seaplane between these two cities. Newspapers followed the trip, and Ruth Nichols became a media sensation. With her blue eyes, dark hair, and lively personality, she became a favorite of reporters. The press called her "Society's Flying Beauty." At first, Nichols felt uncomfortable with the attention, but she soon learned to use publicity to further her goals.

The president of Fairchild Aircraft Corporation, the maker of the seaplane, liked the publicity that surrounded the woman pilot and the attention it brought to his company's plane. He offered her a position in sales. She became the first woman aviator to hold an executive position with a million-dollar aviation company. She flew all over the nation, attending meetings and giving speeches.

With the company's approval, Nichols decided to enter competitive air racing, which gave cash prizes. However, she lacked the money to purchase and maintain a plane. She approached the president of the Crosley Radio Corporation and talked him into letting her use one of his personal planes, a Lockheed Vega, the most advanced light transport plane made at the time. The company would put its name on the plane and gain publicity. She would fly the Lockheed

Vega for most of her competitive flying career.

In August 1929, Nichols entered the first Women's Air Derby, a transcontinental flight from Santa Monica, California, to Cleveland, Ohio. She wore a purple leather flying suit and competed against well-known pilots such as Amelia Earhart and Florence "Pancho" Barnes. In Columbus, Ohio, she hit a tractor left on the air field. She could not finish the race.

The next two years saw Ruth Nichols at the peak of her competitive flying. At the end of 1930, she flew nonstop from Mineola, New York, to Burbank, California, in sixteen hours, establishing a new nonstop transcontinental flight record for women. Her return trip,

Ruth Nichols, wrapped in a fur flying coat, climbs into her Lockheed Vega plane at Roosevelt Field on Long Island in 1930. On this flight to Burbank, California, she broke the transcontinental flight record for women. (AP Photo)

made in thirteen hours, twenty-one minutes, beat the transcontinental flight record Charles Lindbergh had set four months earlier.

In March 1931, Nichols attempted a women's altitude record. At 20,000 feet she had to breathe from a tube which connected to an oxygen tank in the wing. As she climbed upward, the temperature plunged to -60 degrees Fahrenheit. Her tongue froze. But she had established an altitude record of 28,743 feet—nearly five and a half miles above the earth. One month later, she set a speed record of 210.704 miles per hour.

Nichols's aviation advisor felt she now had enough experience to attempt the Atlantic Ocean flight. However, it would take months of careful planning and preparation. She also needed a lot of money. To line up more sponsors, Nichols met with executives in the airline and manufacturing industries. She consulted with Charles Lindbergh about her flight.

The Crosley Radio Corporation president agreed to lend his Lockheed Vega for the journey. Nichols had the plane painted white with gold trim and named it *Akita,* a South Dakota Indian word meaning "to discover" or "to explore." She also had something else she wanted to do before she left; she joined the Society of Friends, also known as the Quakers.

On June 1931, Nichols lifted off from Harbor Grace, New York, bound for Newfoundland, the jumping-off point for flights across the Atlantic. As she approached St. John's, Newfoundland, she realized the runway was

Nichols's borrowed Vega is inspected after the crash in New Brunswick that ended her attempt to cross the Atlantic in the summer of 1931. (AP Photo)

too short to accommodate her large plane. She pulled the plane up and cleared a cliff, but hit the treetops on a second cliff and crashed. Rescuers rushed her to the hospital, where X-rays revealed Nichols had fractured five vertebrae in her back. The doctor told her that it would be a year, if ever, before she could fly again. But something deep within told her to get back into the air. A month after the accident, Nichols flew the repaired *Akita*.

Nichols wanted to build her endurance for another transatlantic try. She decided to make a long-distance flight from Oakland, California, to Chicago, Illinois. She intended to break the women's distance record held by French flier Maryse Bastic, who had flown 1,810 miles nonstop. Wearing a steel corset to brace her back, she made a trial flight run from New York to Burbank, California.

On October 24, 1931, meteorologists predicted good weather eastward along her flying route. Nichols lifted off from Oakland at 5:17 PM Pacific Standard Time. She climbed to 10,000 feet and cleared the Sierra Nevada. The pilot had a strong tail wind and unlimited visibility. As she neared Lake Tahoe in Nevada, she roared along at three hundred miles per hour, an almost unheard-of speed at that time for a heavy plane.

Flying over northern Utah, Nichols felt drowsy and turned on her oxygen, which she sucked through a rubber tube. Her head felt as if it were spinning. She exerted too much back pressure on the control stick, and the plane shot up. She pushed the stick forward in a dive while pulling back on the throttle. The plane steadied at 6,000 feet. Nichols realized she had experienced a near blackout at the higher altitude. "Thank you, God," she said. "That was close, Angel."

At midnight, Nichols cleared the Continental Divide at 16,000 feet. Her eyes grew heavy again, and she fought to stay awake. The horizon disappeared, and then she saw a red streak across the darkness—the dawn of October 25. Her long night was over.

Strong crosswinds blew from the north, making it difficult to keep her plane flying straight. Nichols turned, relying on her compass to keep her on course to Chicago. But she did not see Chicago, only trees. She realized that her compass was incorrect. Where was she? Her next checkpoint was Cleveland, but she missed that, too. She followed a river that led to a small city. A sign on a roof read LOUISVILLE. It was 9:40 AM Central Standard Time in Kentucky.

Nichols calculated her flight. She had spent fourteen hours in the air, ten of them flown in darkness at altitudes of over 15,000 feet. She had covered over 1,950 miles, more than the Frenchwoman had flown, and longer than the distance across the Atlantic Ocean. She had broken the women's distance record. "Okay, Ruth," she said, "you can come down now."

When she landed at the airport, she felt nauseated and exhausted from the stress. Her back pain was excruciating. She could not fall asleep until heated towels and a massage were applied. After four hours of rest, she awoke to congratulatory telegrams and newspaper headlines trumpeting her feat. One read: RUTH NICHOLS BREAKS WOMAN'S DISTANCE RECORD—FLIES WITH BROKEN BACK.

The next morning, Nichols climbed back into the *Akita* for her trip home to New York. As the plane rolled down the runway, the control stick suddenly jerked out of her hand. She stopped and opened the plane's hatch. Smoke filled the cockpit, and flames curled around the fuselage. She heard a mechanic yell, "Get out! GET OUT QUICK! She'll EXPLODE!"

Nichols tried to stand up, but she was wedged in by her parachute, her heavy flight suit, and her steel corset. She struggled to unclasp the buckles of her parachute. Flames licked close to the cockpit. She heard people screaming. Finally, she opened the buckles. Ignoring

This magazine portrait shows Ruth Nichols in her customized purple flight suit.
(The Ninety-Nines, Oklahoma City)

her back pain, she lunged out of the cockpit and out onto a wing. She jumped—and landed on two mechanics. At that instant, the gas tank behind the pilot's seat exploded.

Astonished, Nichols saw the plane's propellers still turning through the smoke. In her panic to exit the plane, she had failed to turn off the ignition. She realized that the whirling blades had created a draft that kept the flames away from the cockpit and allowed her enough time to escape. "Aunty," she whispered, "God did it again."

Once again, Nichols began the intensive planning a transatlantic flight required. In May 1932, in the middle of preparation, she received word that her friend Amelia Earhart had crossed the Atlantic Ocean first. She felt sad but not angry. Later, she wrote in her book, *Wings for Life:*

> That Amelia always seemed to manage to beat me to the starting line in record flight that both of us were planning was simply the fall of the cards. . . . We both won a lot and lost a lot. . . . If Amelia could be here today I am sure that she would join me in saying that the joy is in the race itself, not alone in the victory—and once you have experienced the exaltation of space and speed in flight, no matter who wins, it's mostly velvet.

Nichols did not brood for long. On December 31, 1932, she piloted the first flight of New York and New England Airlines from New York City to Bristol, Connecticut, becoming the first woman airline pilot in United States history. She also served as air-traffic manager for the airline and flew as a reserve pilot.

After the stock market crashed in 1929, the Great Depression took ruthless hold of the nation. Nichols had no money to buy a plane and instead flew private planes belonging to others. During 1933-1934, she lectured at colleges about aviation technology. By 1935, she had begun barnstorming. During one flight, she, with a copilot at the controls, had to make an emergency landing in Troy, New York. Nichols suffered severe injuries in the fiery crash and spent six months recuperating from a dozen fractures. She had to be airlifted back home.

Still, once recovered, Nichols resumed flying and renewed her commercial pilot's license. She committed herself to using aviation to help people, discussing her plans with Aunt Angel. In 1937, Ruth flew fund-raising tours for the Emergency Peace Campaign, a Quaker service committee dedicated to world peace. That same year, her father died. (Aunty lived into her nineties.)

Ever since her 1935 airlift after the accident, Nichols had been thinking about the need for a national air ambulance service to help during disasters. In 1940, she organized Relief Wings, a humanitarian service that airlifted medical personnel and relief workers to disaster areas. "In doing so," she said, "it may be demonstrated that aviation has a heart as well as wings."

Nichols set about raising funds and training volunteers—doctors, nurses, radio operators, and civilian pilots—for emergency airlifts. In 1941, when the United States entered World War II, Nichols folded Relief Wings into the Civil Air Patrol (CAP), a federally funded aviation program. During the war, she served as a nurse's aide and flight instructor.

Nichols sits in the cockpit of her plane before taking off on her trip as an ambassador for UNICEF in July 1949. (AP Photo)

In July 1949, she became an air ambassador for the United Nations International Children's Emergency Fund (UNICEF). She had the assignment of gathering information about needy children in Southeast Asia, India, the Middle East, and Eastern Europe. Nichols mostly flew as a passenger, but the crew of the four-engine D-4 Skymaster let her take the controls periodically.

Carrying her UNICEF reports, she caught a flight from Rome, Italy, back to New York. The pilots overshot a refueling stop in Shannon, Ireland. As they attempted to return, the plane ran out of fuel, and the crew had to ditch in the Irish Sea. Nichols and other passengers drifted in an overturned, overcrowded life raft. She led them in hymns to keep up their spirits. They floated for hours in icy waters before being rescued by a trawler. Ruth Nichols had survived her sixth major crash, this time uninjured.

In the 1950s, Nichols served as aeromedical advisor to the CAP. She made headlines again in 1958 when she piloted a supersonic Delta Dagger to an altitude of 51,000 feet, flying one thousand miles an hour.

Ruth Nichols died September 25, 1960, in her apartment in New York City, at the age of fifty-nine. During her flying career, she had piloted over 140 different models of aircraft and used her aviation skills to serve others. This accomplished woman of flight had successfully melded the two greatest forces in her life—the adventuresome spirit of her father and the compassion of her Quaker aunt.

TIMELINE

1901	Born in New York City on February 23.
1924	Becomes first woman licensed to fly a hydroplane.
1927	Becomes one of the first two women to earn a transport plane license.
1930	Sets a transcontinental speed record for women, flying from Mineola, New York, to Burbank, California, in sixteen hours, fifty-nine minutes; sets a transcontinental speed record of thirteen hours, twenty-one minutes, breaking Charles Lindbergh's record.
1931	On March 6, sets a women's altitude record of 28,743 feet; sets a new women's speed record of 210.704 mph on April 13; crashes in Newfoundland, Canada, while attempting a solo Atlantic flight in June; sets nonstop distance record of 1,977.6 miles, from Oakland, California, to Louisville, Kentucky, in October.
1932	Becomes first woman airline pilot to fly a U.S. commercial airline (New York and New England Airways).
1940	Founder and executive director of Relief Wings, a humanitarian airlift organization.
1948	Appointed special ambassador for the United Nations International Children's Emergency Fund (UNICEF) global air tour.
1958	Sets an altitude record of 51,000 feet, flying one thousand mph in a jet.
1960	Dies in New York City on September 25.

Louise Thaden. (National Archives)

Louise Thaden

COCKPITS AND CAMARADERIE

Almost every pilot who met Louise Thaden liked her. Not only did she have a reputation for being one of the best fliers in the business, but she was also down-to-earth and fun-loving. Her humor and sheer sense of joy attracted people to her. This tall, lean woman possessed a passion for flight and a great capacity for friendship.

Louise was born November 12, 1905, in Bentonville, Arkansas, to Roy and Edna McPhetridge. She had one sister, Alice, who was two years younger. Her father, a farmer, had wanted Louise to be a boy. Growing up, she trailed him everywhere. He taught her to fish and how to repair the family automobile. Later in life, she expressed appreciation that her father had taught her mechanics and, more importantly, sportsmanship.

Louise had wanted to fly for as long as she could remember. At the age of seven, she jumped off the family barn holding a large umbrella. The sustained bruises did not dampen her enthusiasm. When she was fourteen, she took her first plane ride with a barnstormer. She knew she had to learn to fly someday.

She finished Bentonville High School and entered the University of Arkansas at the age of fifteen. Louise first majored in journalism, later switching to physical education. She dropped out of college during her junior year and worked for the J. H. Turner Coal Company in Wichita, Kansas, where she sold coal and fuel oil. She spent her weekends watching planes being built at the Travel Air factory in Wichita. Her employer introduced her to Walter Beech, head of the Travel Air Corporation.

Louise returned to college after a year to work on a pre-medicine degree, but it did not last. She had made up her mind to learn flying. She returned to Wichita to work for the coal company but still spent most of her time at the Travel Air factory. In 1927, Walter Beech offered her a job as sales representative with his Pacific coast distributorship in San Francisco, California. As part of her salary, she would receive free flying lessons. Although her father did not want Louise to fly, he gave her $2,000 before she left.

The twenty-one-year-old had no glamorous job in California. She learned aviation literally from the ground up. She helped assemble planes for customers, sold tickets for air rides, typed, and did anything else that

Louise Thaden with her characteristic expression of confidence, poise, and passion for adventure.

needed to be done. Travel Air gave Louise flying lessons, and she earned her pilot's license in 1927. Her license read No. 74 and was signed by Orville Wright.

Nineteen twenty-eight proved to be an eventful year for the young pilot. She married Herbert Thaden, a former U.S. Army pilot and engineer. On December 7, she attempted a women's altitude record in Oakland, California. For this flight, she made her own oxygen equipment by connecting a rubber hose from a hospital ether mask to an oxygen cylinder. She had to turn the control valve with pliers. Thaden ran the danger of passing out if she turned on too much oxygen or if she turned on too little. She did pass out but revived when her plane plunged to 6,000 feet. She attained an official height of 20,260 feet, although her plane altimeter read over 28,000 feet.

Thaden began to think of herself as a hot pilot—a dangerous attitude. During one flight, she had the controls of an unfamiliar plane. She carried one passenger and another pilot. At four hundred feet, the plane's engine quit, and she tried to turn back to the airport. The plane went into a flat spin, from which it was almost impossible to recover. The aircraft crashed, injuring Thaden and killing her passenger. She blamed her own overconfidence and bad judgment. "Hot salty tears streamed down inside me," she later wrote. A few weeks later, she resumed flying but never forgot her bitter lesson.

She continued to break more flying records. In March 1929, in Oakland, California, she set an endurance flight record of twenty-two hours, three minutes, twelve seconds. In April, piloting a Travel Air plane, she established a speed record, flying 156 miles per hour.

Once Thaden had accumulated two hundred flying hours, she decided to try for her transport plane's license. Her flight examiner said he would be particularly hard on her because she was a woman. Furious, she became determined to prove herself. She became the fourth woman in the United States to earn a transport license.

After two years in California, Thaden made a visit back to Arkansas. The people of Bentonville turned out to greet her. She took her father up for a plane ride. He delighted in the flight and in his daughter, the pilot.

Thaden stopped at the Travel Air factory in Wichita and asked Walter Beech to build her a plane for the National Women's Flying Derby. She almost did not survive the test ride. Up in the air, she experienced light-headedness and nausea. When she landed, she learned that a flaw in the plane's had caused her to experience carbon monoxide poisoning. Beech was able to make adjustments to the plane in time for the race.

The 1929 National Women's Air Derby was the first major air race in which women were allowed to partici-pate. The 3,000-mile course began in Santa Monica, California, and ended in Cleveland, Ohio. The race lasted eight days with sixteen stops, or laps, along the way. Prize money totaled $8,000, plus $200-$500 for the winner of each lap. Twenty women pilots qualified for the race. The entrants included well-known aviators such as Amelia Earhart, Florence "Pancho" Barnes, and Germany's famous stunt pilot Thea Rasche.

Officials had scheduled takeoff for August 18 at 2:00 PM. Thaden walked to her blue-and-gold plane in ner-vous excitement. "This is adventure," she thought. "May we all come safely through." When the official flagged her off, she screamed over the roar of her engine, "I'm away!" Once airborne, her tension disappeared.

The derby did prove to be an adventure. Along the route, the pilots ran into bad weather, developed me-chanical problems, and had to make forced landings. Pancho Barnes and Ruth Nichols crashed and had to quit the race. Another pilot developed typhoid fever. Marvel Crosson never arrived at the stop in Phoenix, Arizona. Searchers found her crumpled plane and her broken body in the desert. Thaden felt saddened by Crosson's death but did not want the race stopped. Neither did the remaining pilots. She wrote, "To us the successful completion of the Derby was of more import [importance] than life or death."

All the way, Thaden flew her plane as hard as she could. Above the desert, she hit an air pocket and smashed her goggles. Flying over Kansas, she ran into a thunderstorm. In the open cockpit, rain hit her skin like stabbing needles. She laughed, thinking, "It is magnificent to be alive! To ride down the lanes of the sky."

One of the stops was at Wichita. Proud Travel Air factory workers whooped and hollered as she zoomed across in first place. A delighted Walter Beech shook her hand. When her parents saw her, they broke into tears.

On August 26, the final day of the race, the pilots landed in Columbus, Ohio, their last stop before Cleveland, 126 miles away. By this time, Thaden had an hour's accumulated flying time over the other pilots. A race official told her to cut back her speed and ease into Cleveland, but she could not bring herself to do it. She flew with the throttle wide open, just as she had done throughout the race.

In Cleveland, Thaden's plane streaked across the finish line at 2 PM. She did not realize that she had won until reporters and photographers surrounded her plane.

With spectators cheering wildly in the background, Thaden is wheeled in her plane to the winner's circle in Cleveland where she will be pronounced the victor of the 1929 National Women's Air Derby. (National Archives)

She had flown the Women's Air Derby in an elapsed flying time of twenty-two hours, three minutes, and twenty-eight seconds. In her victory speech, she said, "I'm glad to be here. All the girls flew a splendid race, much better than I. Each deserves first place, because each is a winner. Mine is a faster ship. Thank you."

The Air Derby was the beginning of lifelong friendships with the other women pilots. Although competitors, they had developed camaraderie, a sense of sharing. All knew they could count on Thaden for help or to share a laugh or two. When Ruth Nichols had to make a forced landing in mountains, she called Thaden for assistance. And Amelia Earhart saw Thaden as a trusted friend. "If Louise ever let's [sic] me down," she said, "I'll never have faith in a human being again."

In 1930, Thaden took a part-time job as director of

the women's division at the Penn School of Aviation. A few months later, Pittsburgh Aviation Industries named her director of public relations. That same year, she had a son. She took baby Bill on his first plane ride at the age of three months.

In July 1932, the manager of Curtiss Airport in Valley Stream, New York, asked Thaden if she would like to pilot a refueling endurance flight with aviator Frances Marsalis. They would attempt to beat the refueling record set in 1931 by Edna May Cooper and Evelyn "Bobbi" Trout. Neither Thaden nor Marsalis knew anything about refueling flights, but it sounded like fun.

After three weeks of practice with the refueling plane, Thaden and Marsalis lifted off on August 12, 1932, flying a Curtiss Thrush. They had to circle Curtiss Air Field, staying in the air long enough to beat the previous record of 123 hours. Although Thaden flew as lead pilot, the two took turns at the controls. Marsalis had the responsibility of handling the refuelings and food drops.

Gasoline, supplies, and food had to come from the refueling plane, a smaller Curtiss Robin. Fuel flowed from the refueler to the Thrush by means of a rubber hose. Food, correspondence, and newspapers were dropped in a weighted bucket. It took great skill on the part of the pilots in both the Robin and the Thrush to maneuver and remain in position while making contact. The first three efforts proved successful. On the second day, a food bucket tore the fabric on a wing. Thaden had to bring down the plane for repairs. The duo would have to start over again.

They ascended a second time on August 14, wishing they could be anywhere else, doing anything else but this. After three days, they developed sore throats from shouting over the engine noise. Their hands grew stiff. Their air mattress sprang a leak. To stay awake, they whistled, sang, and slapped each other on the back. Still, they continued to fly around and around and around. No, this was not fun.

About midway in their merry-go-round flight, they received a note from the airport manager saying that reporters on the ground had complained about the dullness of watching the plane circling endlessly overhead. How about if Marsalis developed an "appendicitis attack" in the air? The hoax would be a secret among the three of them. The two women looked at each other and shrugged. "Oh well," they said, "why not?" The refueler dropped ice and medical supplies. The next day, Thaden reported that Marsalis felt "much better," and that they would continue. The two brave women pilots made newspaper headlines. (Coincidentally, a week later, Thaden suffered a real appendicitis attack.)

On August 20th, Thaden and Marsalis surpassed Cooper and Trout's 123-hour record. The two women flew for two more days until fatigue and boredom finally forced them down on August 22. The pilots had flown 17,000 miles over eight days. They had stayed aloft 196 hours, 5 minutes and had set a new women's refueling endurance record.

In 1935, Thaden's good friend Phoebe Omlie, who worked for the Bureau of Air Commerce, asked her to join the National Air Marking Program. This government-sponsored program had as its goal to establish ground markers across the United States as navigational aids to pilots. The other pilots in on the team included Helen Richey, Helen McCloskey, Nancy Harkness, and Blanche Noyes. They marked states off in grids, establishing markers at intersections. The name of the nearest town would be painted on the roof of the most prominent building. If the intersection fell in an isolated area, painted rocks marked the spot. The hardest work came in trying to talk state officials into actually participating in this project.

Thaden and Blanche Noyes took two weeks off from the National Air Marking Program to prepare for flying the 1936 Bendix Trophy Race, one of the most prestigious aviation racing events. Sponsors of the cross-country race had opened it to women for the first time. Amelia Earhart, Helen Richey, and Laura Ingalls also entered. The transcontinental route went from New York to California. Walter Beech's wife, Olive Ann, talked her husband (who had designed a new line of planes) into sponsoring Thaden and Noyes. He gave them a commercial plane right off the assembly line, a Beech C17R Staggerwing. All the other pilots entered in the Derby had planes built specifically for racing.

On September 3, at 4:30 AM, Thaden and Noyes lifted off from Bennett Field, New York. Thaden piloted the

Thaden's copilot in the 1936 Bendix Trophy Race, Blanche Noyes.

Staggerwing; Noyes served as navigator and copilot. They ran into problems almost immediately. The radio ceased working, depriving the pilots of critical weather reports. They ran into fog and became lost. When they managed to get under the cloud cover, they were delighted to spot one of their own air markers.

Flying over Kansas, they ran into storms. Winds buffeted the Staggerwing. When they landed at Wichita to refuel, Walter Beech expressed impatience at the pace of their flying. He told Thaden to open the throttle, but she flew the plane at a cruising speed all the way to California.

Coming into Los Angeles, Noyes asked, "Do you know where the airport is?" Thaden thought she knew. Finally they spied the airport, but the finish line happened to be on an adjacent field. Thaden felt certain they would be the last pilots to arrive, but she roared across the white finish line anyway. Again, she did not know they had won until people surrounded the plane. Louise Thaden had flown the 1936 Bendix Trophy Race in an elapsed time of fourteen hours and fifty-five minutes. (Laura Ingalls arrived forty-five minutes later to capture second place; Amelia Earhart and Helen Richey came in fifth.) The sponsor of the race handed Louise the grand trophy and gave the two women $7,000 in prize money. A tearful Olive Ann Beech hugged them.

As a result of winning the Bendix, Louise Thaden was awarded the 1936 Harmon Trophy, the highest honor given to any female pilot. In her acceptance speech she gave much credit to her copilot Blanche Noyes. Then Thaden continued making records. Within the next year, she had set another speed record of 197.958 miles per hour at St. Louis, Missouri.

A restored Beech Staggerwing, painted according to the 1936 Sherwin-Williams Airplane Finishing Specifications. It has the exact markings on the cowling that Louise Thaden had on her C17R model Beech for the 1936 Bendix Trophy Race.

In 1938, Thaden retired from competitive racing to devote more time to her family. (A daughter had been born three years earlier.) Walter Beech offered her a job demonstrating his company's planes, and she worked many years for the Beech Aircraft Corporation.

A German U-boat off the eastern coastline of the United States flees from a Civil Air Patrol aircraft. The pilots who flew these missions were called subchasers, providing homeland defense using civil aviation resources. (CAP)

During World War II, Thaden joined Ruth Nichols in the Civil Air Patrol (CAP), advancing to the rank of lieutenant colonel. After the war, she continued to support aviation and the aircraft industry through her writing and speeches. She also later flew a glider and a jet plane.

Louise Thaden died November 9, 1979, in High Point, North Carolina, three days shy of her 74th birthday. Through the years, women aviators have continued to pay tribute to this groundbreaking pilot. When astronaut Eileen Collins flew the 1991 space shuttle, she carried Louise Thaden's flight helmet onboard.

TIMELINE

1905	Born in Bentonville, Arkansas, on November 12.
1927	Receives her pilot's license, # 74, signed by Orville Wright.
1928	Sets a women's altitude record of 20,260 feet.
1929	Establishes a women's endurance record of twenty-two hours, three minutes, twelve seconds in Oakland, California; sets speed record of 156 mph; earns transport plane license; wins the National Women's Air Derby.
1930	Appointed director of the women's division of the Penn School of Aviation.
1932	Sets a women's refueling endurance record at Valley Stream, New York.
1935	Works with the National Air Marking Program.
1936	Becomes first woman pilot to win the Bendix Trophy Race; is named recipient of the Harmon Trophy.
1937	Sets women's speed record of 197.958 mph in St. Louis, Missouri.
1942	Serves in the Civil Air Patrol.
1979	Dies in High Point, North Carolina, on November 9.

Anne Morrow Lindbergh. (Library of Congress)

Anne Morrow Lindbergh

AVIATOR, WRITER

R eaders in the 1930s knew Anne Morrow Lindbergh as the woman who wrote about the magic of flying. Other people thought of her as the wife of a famous aviator or as the mother of an infamously kidnapped child. Far fewer realized that she had set a number of flight records and was a valued aviator in her own right.

On June 22, 1906, Elizabeth and Dwight Morrow of Englewood, New Jersey, welcomed the birth of their second girl, Anne Spencer. The wealthy parents gave their four children the best of everything, including fine schools and frequent trips to Europe. Anne saw little of her financier father, but she felt close to her mother.

Anne was small, pretty, and bookish. She worried she did not measure up to her two outgoing sisters and her energetic mother. However, she could write. She knew from an early age that she wanted to be a writer, and her family encouraged her efforts. She won two literary awards while attending Smith College in Northampton, Massachusetts.

Anne was at Smith when President Calvin Coolidge appointed her father as ambassador to Mexico. In 1927, she went to Mexico City to spend Christmas with her family. Dwight Morrow had invited aviator Charles A. Lindbergh to be his guest at the embassy. Six months earlier, Lindbergh had made a nonstop solo flight from New York to France and became an international hero. At first, Anne felt annoyed that this man had intruded on the family gathering, but when she met him at dinner, she found him to be shy and unassuming—and intriguing.

After graduating from Smith College in 1928, Anne Morrow joined her family in Mexico and saw Lindbergh again. Reporters and photographers hounded their steps. Charles took her up in his Curtiss biplane and let her take the controls while airborne. She said, "Never have I had such a wonderful feeling of escape as when we left the ground."

On May 27, 1929, Anne and Charles married secretly at her parents' home. As the wife of one of the most famous people in the world, her life would never be easy. But she said, "He opened the door to 'real life,' and although it frightened me, it also beckoned. I had to go."

In January 1930, the couple flew to San Diego, California, where Charles wanted to try the new glider plane

Charles Lindbergh had become an American hero when he successfully flew his plane, The Spirit of St. Louis, *from Roosevelt Field, New York, to Paris, in 1927.* (Courtesy of the Granger Collection.)

designed by Hawley Bowlus. (Bowlus had supervised the construction of *The Spirit of St. Louis,* which Lindbergh flew on his solo transatlantic flight.) Anne decided to try gliding after her husband received his glider pilot's license.

She began her lessons by guiding a trainer glider on the ground. A car pulled the glider, while Bowlus bellowed instructions through a megaphone. After she had mastered the controls, she was ready for her solo flight. A car towed the plane to Mt. Soledad, an eight hundred-foot mountain outside San Diego. The glider had long, tapering silver wings that stretched almost sixty-two feet from tip to tip. It had neither engine nor landing wheels, only a boat-like keel on its belly.

Anne sat perched in the glider on the edge of the mountain while men held the glider with bungee cord.

They released the glider, and she became airborne. Soaring down, Anne could feel the columns of air beneath her, and as she neared the ground, she could hear a bird singing. She wrote to her mother, "It was so delicious, so still."

Anne had stayed aloft for six minutes, the time required to earn a license. On January 29, 1930, she became the first woman in the United States to earn a glider pilot's license and the tenth person in the United States to do so. Inspired, area women took up gliding and formed the Anne Lindbergh Glider Club, although its namesake had no personal connection to the group. Of all her experiences in aviation, gliding remained her favorite because of its quietness, and because it gave her the sensation of flying like a bird.

During the 1930s, Charles Lindbergh worked as a consultant to commercial airlines. The president of Pan American Airways wanted to determine possible air routes across the oceans to Asia, Europe, and South America. Lindbergh would plan and pilot these survey routes, but he could not make the flights alone. He needed a copilot, a navigator who would plot the plane's course, and a radio operator who would gather weather information from ground stations. He turned to Anne to fill these roles. Although unsure of her abilities, she set about learning these important aviation skills.

Twice a day, a navigator came to the Lindbergh home to instruct both of them. Anne learned how to determine a plane's position and how to plot a plane's course. She

FLY TO SOUTH SEA ISLES

PAN AMERICAN WORLD AIRWAYS
The System of the Flying Clippers

With the help of the Lindberghs, Pan American began flying aircrafts called Clippers (a reference to the nineteenth-century passenger ships) to south Asia and other intercontinental destinations in the 1930s. (Library of Congress)

became proficient in using a compass and a sextant. She found navigation to be interesting, though time consuming. It was not hard work.

Learning to operate a radio system proved more difficult. Since voice radio was not widely available on planes at the time, she had to use a telegraph radio. To communicate via telegraph, Anne learned Morse Code, a series of dots and dashes that stand for letters of the alphabet. She had to be able to send and receive fifteen words a minute to get her radio license. In addition, she needed to understand electrical and radio theories and pass a written exam. The Lindberghs learned together, and both received their radio operator licenses.

On April 20, 1930, piloting a Lockheed Sirius, Charles and Anne flew from Los Angeles to New York in fourteen hours, twenty-three minutes, and twenty-seven sec-

Charles and Anne Lindbergh in the early years of their marriage. (Library of Congress)

onds—setting a new transcontinental speed record. Anne served as radio operator and navigator. During the entire flight, she felt ill, but did not tell her husband. Two months later, on her twenty-fourth birthday, Anne Lindbergh gave birth to her first child, Charles Lindbergh Jr.

In 1931, Anne Lindbergh learned to fly a powered plane, with her husband as instructor. It was not pleasant working with a perfectionist. If she had a bad landing, he demanded she do it over and over until she did it right.

As with most of their ventures, he pushed her constantly, but she gained confidence. After ten solo flights, she qualified for her pilot's license. Her husband later told his daughter that Anne proved to be as good a pilot as he was.

The Lindberghs began planning their first major flight overseas to chart possible commercial routes to the Far East. They would fly from the United States to Asia, going by way of Canada and Alaska. Such a route would be faster and cheaper than flying westward across the Pacific Ocean. Anne would go as copilot and radio navigator. She left their baby in the care of her mother.

They flew the same Lockheed Sirius as before, which had been outfitted with the pontoons necessary for a water landing. The pontoons also held extra gas tanks with enough fuel to carry them 2,000 miles. In addition to their regular flying equipment, they stowed emergency supplies on board, including a rubber sailboat with an extra radio.

On July 27, 1931, they lifted off from Long Island, New York. After stopping at her parents' summer home in Maine to say good-bye to little Charles, they turned northwest. Anne sent their position every fifteen minutes to ground radio stations. She always felt relief when she received dot-dash-dot (the letter "r"), meaning "received ok." When they stopped in Ottawa, Canada, other pilots tried to discourage Charles from flying over northern Canada. One said, "I wouldn't take my wife into that territory." Charles replied, "You must remember that she is crew."

The Sirius had dual controls that could be operated by either pilot or copilot. Anne sat in the copilot's seat, directly behind her husband. From her cockpit, she could easily reach all of her radio equipment. The radio receiver sat on her right. Since it was bolted to the plane floor, she had to bend over to see and adjust the dials. Wires ran from the radio to the earphones, clamped to her head by her helmet. A coil attached to a radio antenna went through a hole in the plane floor and trailed behind in the air. She hand-cranked the antenna in and out every time she changed frequencies. Receiving messages from radio operators along the way was the most difficult part of her job. She translated the dots and dashes into letters,

Anne (rear seat) *and Charles in the cockpit of their Lockheed Sirius, shortly before takeoff on their trip to Asia.* (Courtesy of Getty Images.)

wrote the letters on a pad, and strung them together to form words.

She sent telegraph messages with a transmitter key about the size of a large, round button. The key was wired to a transmitter box to her left. Another set of coils had to be connected to the transmitter box and the antenna. She juggled her duties constantly. Plug in receiving coils. Adjust the radio dials. Jot down incoming messages. Change coils and transmit back. If static or silence, then reel in the antenna and change the coils to catch another wave frequency and a different radio station.

They flew across Canada to Alaska, over Siberia in the Soviet Union, and down to Japan. At stops, Anne mailed letters back home, inquiring about the baby. In one letter to her mother, she wrote, "I like everything you tell me about his playing, exploring your room while you write at your desk . . . and crawling over the lawn with his blocks. And describing his curls coming out from his blue cap."

From Japan, they went on to China, where they viewed the great yellow Yantze River, which was flooding much of the country at that time. A relief agency asked the Lindberghs to survey the flood damage because they had the only plane capable of flying long distances. Anne flew the plane while Charles drew the maps. Their most frightening moment occurred at Nanking, when starving Chinese flood victims swamped their plane and it almost sank.

After they returned home, on March 1, 1932, the Lindberghs suffered the greatest tragedy of their lives. A kidnapper stole eighteen-month-old Charles Jr. from his bed and left a note demanding money for the child's return. Searchers found the baby's body on May 12. The whole nation followed the kidnapping story, and people mourned the child's death with the Lindberghs.

Anne's second son, Jon, was born three months later. Although she felt relief that the new baby was healthy, this happy event could not erase the unbearable memory of losing her firstborn. Two years later, police arrested Bruno Hauptmann for the kidnapping and murder of little Charles. A jury found Hauptmann guilty, and he was executed.

In 1933, the Lindberghs prepared to make an aerial survey of possible commercial routes across the Atlantic Ocean. Anne Lindbergh hated the thought of leaving her son for five-and-a-half months, even though she knew he would be well cared for by her mother. However, her role as radio operator would be even more critical on this trip because they would be flying over vast distances of ice and water. Charles Lindbergh considered this 30,000-mile journey to be even more hazardous than his 1927 flight across the Atlantic.

On July 9, 1933, they left Long Island, New York, for Greenland, stopping first in Canada. Much of Greenland had not been surveyed because of the mountain ranges and the solid ice cap that covered its interior. They crisscrossed the ice cap twice and charted unknown mountains. As they landed at coastal villages, Greenlanders greeted them with shouts of "Ting-miss-ar-toq—Ting-miss-ar-toq!" The Lindberghs called their plane *Tingmissartoq,* meaning "the one who flies like a big bird." It now hangs in the National Air & Space Museum in Washington, DC.

The Lindberghs spent the summer months of 1933 in Greenland and Iceland. During the fall, they went to Scandinavia, the Soviet Union, central Europe, and the United Kingdom. With winter approaching, they would not be able to fly back across the northern Atlantic. They decided to take a southerly route to Africa, cross the Atlantic Ocean to South America, then turn north toward the United States.

On December 6, the *Tingmissartoq* lifted off from Bathhurst, Gambia, at 2:00 AM and headed toward Natal, Brazil. The 1,800-mile journey across the Atlantic Ocean would take sixteen hours, but they would have only twelve hours of daylight. Anne began trying to establish contact with South American radio stations to get critical weather information. On they flew through the darkness, going through clouds that hid the stars by which she usually navigated. Another worry came when the sextant malfunctioned. While Charles fixed the sextant, she piloted the plane, keeping on her headphones to hear any incoming messages.

Several hours into daylight, they spied ships on the ocean. Anne made radio contact with one. Charles veered off course and headed in the ship's direction. As the plane roared down, Anne could see men on deck waving at them. Had she not always said that communication was the greatest thing in the world? She waved frantically back.

The Lindberghs set down safely at Natal, Brazil, at 6:00 PM. They decided to make a trip up the Amazon River before continuing up the coast toward home. They arrived back in the United States on December 19, 1938, just in time for Christmas. In her book of essays, *Moon Shine,* she wrote:

> We shall not cease from exploration
> And the end of all our exploring
> Will be to arrive where we started
> And know the place for the first time.

Anne Lindbergh now began writing about her first two transoceanic flights. *North to the Orient,* about their journey to Asia, was published in 1935. Her book about the Atlantic trip, *Listen! the Wind,* came out three years later. People reading her books remarked that it was just like being in the cockpit with her. Charles had always admired her writing and pushed her to do more.

Between 1937 and 1945, Anne had four more children: Land, Anne, Scott, and Reeve. The Lindberghs fought fiercely for their children's privacy and moved the family to rural Connecticut. Charles traveled most of the time, while Anne managed the household, looked after the children, and wrote. Charles warned the children not to interrupt their mother when she was at her desk, but they did, and she never seemed to mind.

Anne Morrow Lindbergh at her home in Darien, Connecticut, in 1956. (Courtesy of Getty Images.)

The Lindberghs experienced dark times in the late 1930s and early 1940s. Charles feared the strength of

German air forces and urged the United States to remain out of the upcoming war. He came under withering criticism for remarks that appeared to be pro-Nazi and anti-Jewish. Anne reviewed his writings and warned him about his choice of words, but he did not listen.

After flying combat missions in the Pacific during World War II, Charles Lindbergh retreated from public life. Anne Morrow Lindbergh continued her writing, publishing fourteen books in all. None of her later works dealt directly with aviation.

During the 1960s and 1970s, Anne and Charles Lindbergh became active in environmental causes. They worked with the World Wildlife Fund and traveled to Africa and the Philippines. Anne marveled at the images of the beautiful blue earth beamed from space. "Through the eyes of the astronauts," she wrote, "we have seen more clearly than ever before this precious earth essence that must be preserved."

In 1974, Charles Lindbergh passed away on the island of Maui, Hawaii. Anne Morrow Lindbergh died in Vermont on February 7, 2001, at the age of ninety-five. She had participated in the great aviation ventures of the twentieth century. And she had communicated the sensations of flight to millions. Few did it better.

TIMELINE

1906	Born in Englewood, New Jersey, on June 22.
1929	Marries Charles A. Lindbergh.
1930	Becomes first woman in United States to earn glider pilot's license; serves as navigator and radio operator on Charles Lindbergh's transcontinental flight.
1931	Earns private pilot's license; flies on survey of air routes to Asia.
1932	Charles Lindbergh Jr. is kidnapped on March 1; found dead on May 12.
1933	Flies as copilot, navigator, and radio operator on transatlantic survey journey; becomes the first woman to cross both the Atlantic and Pacific oceans.
1934	Becomes the first woman to win the National Geographic Society's Hubbard Gold Medal.
1979	Elected to the National Aviation Hall of Fame.
2001	Dies in Vermont on February 7.

Jackie Cochran. (National Archives)

Jacqueline Cochran

TEST PILOT

J ackie Cochran lived her life at full throttle, just as she flew. She possessed enormous energy and extraordinary determination. When she set her mind to do something, she would not be stopped. She sought risk and excitement. "Adventure was always around the corner," she said, "and I could turn that corner mighty fast."

In her autobiography, Jackie Cochran explained that she did not know her exact date of birth or her birth name, though relatives claim she was born Bessie Pittman on May 11, 1906. She wrote that she grew up in northern Florida with a foster family that moved frequently from one sawmill camp to another.

There is no doubt that Jackie was raised in poverty. She had no shoes until she was eight. She dropped out of school after the second grade, Throughout her life, she had childlike, scrawly handwriting. But she had a sharp mind and learned quickly. From an early age, she never thought of herself as ordinary.

At the age of eight, Jackie worked in a Georgia textile mill. When she was eleven, she started work in a beauty shop. During her teens, she took nursing courses for a while but could not pass the written exam. She went back to the beauty business and eventually became co-owner of a beauty shop. While working in Pensacola, Florida, she picked her name, Jacqueline Cochran, out of a phone book because she liked the way it sounded.

In 1929, she sold her business partnership and moved to New York City, where she worked for a Fifth Avenue beauty salon that catered to the wealthy. During the winter season, she followed her clients to Miami, Florida. There, she met Floyd Odlum, a multimillionaire financier. When she told him of her ambitious plans to start a cosmetics company, he said that she needed to learn to fly in order to market her products widely.

In the summer of 1932, during her vacation, Cochran started her pilot training at Roosevelt Field, Long Island. She tackled flying the way she did everything—with terrier-like tenacity. She earned her pilot's license in three weeks, normally a two-to-three-month process. The following year, she received her commercial pilot's license. In 1934, she took instruction in flying a plane by instruments. She took all of the written exams orally.

In October 1934, Cochran entered her first major

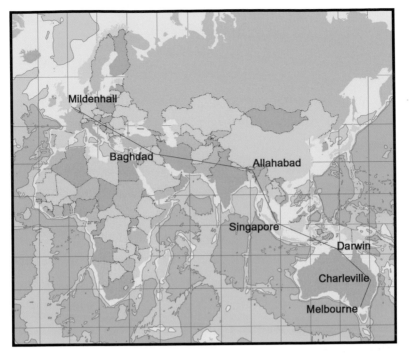

Compulsory stops in the 1934 MacRobertson Air Race.

flying event, the MacRobertson Race, a route that stretched from England to Australia. She flew an experimental plane called the Gee Bee. Built for speed, it had a tendency to overheat and vibrate during flight. She and her copilot experienced mechanical difficulties and put down in Romania. She could not finish the race.

Cochran became obsessed with winning the Bendix Trophy Transcontinental Race, a 2,042-mile run from Los Angeles, California, to Cleveland, Ohio. Not only was it the most prestigious aerial race in this country, but it also paid the largest amount of money to the winners. She had planned to participate in the 1934 Bendix, but her plane blew up in the factory.

Cochran, along with Amelia Earhart, did enter the 1935 Bendix. Once more, Cochran flew the dangerous Gee Bee. When fog rolled in before takeoff, the manufacturer asked her not to fly. She consulted Floyd Odlum and decided to take the risk, even though it might mean death. "If you ponder such possibilities too long or too often," she said, "you'll never risk anything. And to live without risk for me would have been tantamount to death."

Flying over Arizona, she saw storms ahead. Then the Gee Bee started to vibrate. She prepared to land by dumping nearly all of her six hundred gallons of fuel, some of which was sucked back into the cockpit. Gasoline soaked her leather flying suit. She prayed that when she landed a spark would not ignite into flames. When she did land, she tore out of the cockpit and out of her wet flying suit. Rather than criticize the plane's performance, she said, "I just got tired and quit."

In 1935, she started a company, Jacqueline Cochran's Cosmetics, located in New York City. She called her cosmetics line "Wings to Beauty" and painted the slogan on the side of her business plane. (She also painted the number thirteen, which she considered her lucky number.) This blonde beauty, with flawless skin and big, brown eyes, was the best walking advertisement for her own products. She wore the finest of fashions.

A year later, Cochran married Floyd Odlum and finally had the lifestyle she had always wanted. They had three residences: a large apartment in New York City, a country estate in Connecticut, and a ranch in Indio, California. She did her own decorating. At her ranch house, she had a giant fireplace made from uranium rock

Jackie Cochran's husband, lawyer and industrialist Floyd Bostwick Odlum. (Library of Congress)

and lamps ten times normal size. Cochran and her husband enjoyed entertaining the rich and famous.

Amelia Earhart and her husband spent time at the ranch. Cochran adored Earhart, one of the few women she truly liked and admired. Cochran and Odlum helped finance Earhart's around-the-world trip. When Amelia Earhart disappeared over the Pacific Ocean in 1937, Cochran grieved. She saw herself as Earhart's rightful successor as the most famous woman pilot in the world, and she set about proving it.

That same year, Jackie Cochran set three speed records: the women's national speed record (203.895 miles per hour); the women's world speed record (292.271 mph); and a speed record flying from New York to Miami, Florida (four hours, twelve minutes). For these achievements, she was awarded the 1937 Harmon Trophy, given to the most outstanding woman pilot of the year. She also flew the Bendix Race again in 1937, coming in third.

When Cochran entered the 1938 Bendix Race, she was the only woman pilot among nine men. As the owner of a large cosmetics firm, she did not need the prize money, but she did need to win. She flew a new Seversky P-35, an early military pursuit, or fighter, plane. One general told her that she had no business flying this plane because it was a "killer." Cochran ignored the comment. She had chosen the P-35 exactly for its speed. Cochran liked to fly hot, tricky planes, and she liked to compete against men.

The P-35 arrived from the factory only two days before the race. Cochran did not test fly the plane because she feared something might go wrong and she would be disqualified. She would test the P-35 along the way. Before her takeoff, she sat inside the cockpit until she memorized the instrument panel and could touch every dial and gauge while blindfolded.

On September 3, Cochran walked to her plane, which was fully loaded with fuel. The P-35 came equipped with three gas tanks, one in the belly and one in each wing. The aviator climbed into her plane and waited for her 3:00 AM takeoff. She trained her eye on the electric light at the end of the field and opened the throttle. The P-35 cleared the ground at about the halfway mark of the runway.

Once in the air, she switched off the belly gas tank (because it threw the plane off its center of gravity) and switched to the wing tanks, which drained to the engine in tandem. She flew at 16,000 feet with partially open throttle. By doing this, she calculated that she would arrive in Cleveland with twenty gallons of gas left.

Flying over Arizona, Cochran ran into a storm. She climbed to 25,000 feet to get above it. Up that high, she had to breathe from an oxygen tube because the plane was not pressurized. Ice began coating the cockpit windshield, so she brought the plane down to melt the ice. She had lost her radio antenna during takeoff and flew the entire way with no radio contact.

Suddenly at 23,000 feet, the engine quit. Cochran switched to the belly tank to restart the engine. The right wing started to dip, and the plane fell into a spiral. She pulled the P-35 into a shallow dive to bring it out of the deadly spin. The plane had dropped several thousand feet.

The right wing still hung heavy, which indicated that its fuel tank remained full. Cochran tipped the plane over on its left wing, causing fuel to drain from the full right wing to the empty left wing. She flew the remainder of the trip rocking the plane from side to side. An inspection later showed that a wad of paper had clogged the right-wing fuel line.

When Cochran passed over St. Mary's Lakes in Ohio, she knew she was not far from her goal. She had her throttle wide open. She went so fast that she passed the Cleveland airport, so she turned around and landed on the opposite side. Jackie Cochran had flown 2,042 miles in 8 hours, 10 minutes, and 31 seconds, at an average speed of 249.774 miles per hour. When she landed, she had less than three minutes supply of fuel left. "Did I have guts," she later said.

Race officials rode out to the runway to meet her, but Cochran kept them waiting while she combed her hair and put on fresh makeup. Vincent Bendix, aircraft manufacturer and sponsor of the race, greeted the new champion. For forty minutes, she shook hands and posed for photographs. Then the Bendix winner climbed back into her refueled plane and headed east.

Vincent Bendix congratulates Cochran on her record-breaking win of the 1938 Bendix Trophy. (Smithsonian Institution)

She continued on to Bendix Airport, New Jersey. Jackie Cochran had flown from one end of the United States to the other in ten hours, twenty-seven minutes, and fifty seconds—a new transcontinental record. She caught an airliner back to Cleveland to pick up her Bendix trophy.

In 1939, she set even more aviation records. In March, she tried for an altitude record, flying a Beechcraft Staggerwing. Sucking on an oxygen tube, she went up to 33,000 feet in an unpressurized cockpit. Suddenly, she felt dizzy. In setting her altitude record, she had ruptured a blood vessel in her sinuses. Cochran flew for about an hour around the airport, trying to get her bearings before landing. Later, during the summer, she broke two speed records. On August 8th, 1939, she became the first woman to make a landing by instrument only.

In September 1939, Germany invaded Poland and started World War II in Europe. Cochran wrote a letter to First Lady Eleanor Roosevelt, saying that if the United States ever went to war, she knew women pilots in this country could help. Initially, the United States remained neutral in the conflict, although it provided planes and other aid to Great Britain, France, and the Soviet Union.

To dramatize Great Britain's war plight, Cochran flew a Lockheed Hudson bomber across the Atlantic Ocean on June 17, 1941. When she returned to the United States in July, President Roosevelt asked her to draw up a plan for using women pilots. Cochran and her staff culled aviation records and found over 2,500 women pilots who held private pilot's licenses. In her plan, Cochran proposed putting civilian women pilots through the same military flight training as the men. These trained women would ferry military aircraft from the manufacturers to bases or to port cities within the continental United States. The military turned down her proposal, saying women pilots were not needed.

Cochran was asked to head up a group of American women pilots that would help transport military planes from factories to bases within the United Kingdom. She selected twenty-five commercially licensed women pilots. For eighteen months, they ferried planes for the British Air Transport Auxiliary. These women became known as the American "ATA girls."

On December 7, 1941, the Japanese attacked Pearl Harbor in Honolulu, Hawaii, and the United States declared war. The military did not have enough trained male pilots to fly combat overseas and ferry planes. The Army Air Forces turned to women pilots to help. In September 1942, Jackie Cochran's proposal for training civilian women pilots was accepted. She was appointed as head of the Women's Flying Training Detachment (WFTD). Two months later, the women pilots started their training in Houston, Texas. The WFTD made a final move to Avenger Field in Sweetwater, Texas, and became the only all-women military base in United States history.

In September 1942, a group of twenty-eight women pilots called the Women's Auxiliary Ferrying Squadron

Jackie Cochran in her WASP uniform in the 1940s.

(WAFS) was organized by Nancy Love, another notable aviator. This elite group of women pilots held commercial licenses. With an average of over 1,100 flying hours each, they needed only a limited amount of training to ferry military planes.

In 1943, the two groups of women pilots combined to form the Women Airforce Service Pilots (WASP), which remained a civilian auxiliary to the Army Air Forces. Cochran assumed the role as director of all women pilots. She set about expanding the roles of women pilots to include towing targets for gunnery practice, testing repaired planes, and other duties. With her outsized ego and insistence on doing things her way, she alienated many in the military establishment and even some of her own pilots. Others admired her guts and vision.

As the Allies ground on toward victory in World War II, the Army Air Forces shut down the women's training program, and the WASP disbanded. Before the band of pilots deactivated in December 1944, they had flown over six million miles in the more than seventy different military planes made at the time. Thirty-eight women in this organization died in service to their country.

Jackie Cochran did not look back. She became a reporter for *Liberty* magazine and witnessed the surrender of the Japanese in 1945. She also attended the Nuremberg trials in Germany, where Nazi leaders went on trial for war crimes. In 1945, she received the United States Distinguished Service Medal for her wartime service. After the war, she lobbied for the creation of the U.S. Air Force (established in 1947) and became a consultant to this new branch of the Defense Department.

During the 1950s, she flew as a test pilot for two aircraft industries. On May 20, 1953, at Edwards Air Base in California, she broke the sound barrier flying a Northrop Sabrejet F-86, becoming the first woman to accomplish this feat. Chuck Yeager, the first person to break the sound barrier in 1947, instructed her. He said about Cochran, "She was tough and bossy and used to getting her own way." He also said she was a superb pilot.

Cochran continued testing military planes into her fifties. In 1962, she set nine international altitude, speed, and distance records in the F-86. She broke two more speed records in 1963, flying a Lockheed F-104G Starfighter, one of the most dangerous planes ever made. On May 4, 1963, she pushed the Starfighter to 1,429 miles per hour and became the first woman pilot to go twice the speed of sound.

Cochran and her husband funded research in aviation

Test pilot and World War II flying ace Chuck Yeager stands next to Jackie Cochran, seated in her plane. Both pilots earned lasting fame for breaking the sound barrier. (Air Force photograph)

medicine. She also advocated training women to become astronauts. Like most of the programs she had proposed for women pilots, she thought women should train separately from men—and she wanted to be a part of this program. But her ideas did not fly with the Air Force or with women pilots.

During the 1970s, Cochran's health suffered. In 1971, she was inducted into the Aviation Hall of Fame in Dayton, Ohio, the first woman to be so honored. After her husband died in 1974, her health deteriorated further.

Jackie Cochran died in Indio, California, on August 19, 1980, at the age of seventy-four. She had set over two hundred flying records, more than any pilot in U.S. aviation history. This test pilot had found—and created—enough adventure to last several lifetimes. "Adventure is a state of mind—and spirit," she said. "It comes with faith, for with complete faith there is no fear of what faces you in life or death."

TIMELINE

1906	Born in northern Florida on May 11.
1932	Earns her pilot's license.
1933	Earns her commercial pilot's license.
1935	Starts Jacqueline Cochran's Cosmetics, Inc.
1937	Sets three major speed records.
1938	Wins the Bendix Trophy Transcontinental Race; honored with Harmon Trophy.
1939	Becomes first woman to make an instruments-only landing.
1941	Becomes first woman to fly a bomber plane across the Atlantic Ocean; recruits twenty-five U.S. women pilots to serve in the British Air Transport Auxiliary.
1942	Creates the Women's Flying Training Detachment.
1943	Becomes director of Women Airforce Service Pilots (WASP).
1945	Receives the United States Distinguished Service Medal.
1953	Becomes first woman to break the sound barrier.
1962	Sets nine international records in speed and altitude.
1964	Flies twice the speed of sound in a Lockheed F-104 Starfighter.
1971	Becomes first woman to be inducted into the Aviation Hall of Fame.
1980	Dies in Indio, California, on August 9.

sources

HARRIET QUIMBY

p. 12, "bird-men heroes," Henry Holden and Lori Griffin, *Ladybirds II: The Continuing Story of American Women in Aviation* (Mount Freedom, NJ: Black Hawk Publishing Company, 1993), 8.

p. 12, "In my opinion . . ." Valerie Moolman, *Women Aloft* (Alexandria, VA: Time-Life Books, 1981), 23.

p. 15-16, "I removed my goggles . . ." Ibid., 3-4.

p. 18, "Only a cautious person . . ." Jean Adams and Margaret Kimball, *Heroines of the Sky* (Freeport, NY: Books for Libraries, 1970), 22.

p. 21, "Good luck!" Terry Gywnn-Jones, "For a Brief Moment the World Seemed Wild About Harriet," *Smithsonian* (January 1984), 120.

KATHERINE STINSON

p. 27, "Be careful, now . . ." Charles Planck, *Women with Wings* (New York: Harper and Brothers, 1942), 27.

p. 31, "Fear, as I understand it . . ." "Katherine Stinson, the Flying Schoolgirl," *FAA Aviation News* (November 1971), 11.

p. 35, "Banzai," "San Antonio Aviatrix Captures Japan; Katherine Stinson Thrills Nipponese," *San Antonio Express* (September 28, 1917), 1.

p. 35, "How waiting we were . . ." John Underwood, *The Stinsons* (Glendale, CA: Heritage Press), 14.

p. 36, "Miss Shih Lien Sun . . ." Debra Weingarten, *Katherine Stinson: The Flying Schoolgirl* (Austin, TX: Eakin Press, 2000), 64.

p. 39, "It seems to me so simple . . ." Ibid., 28.

RUTH LAW

p. 41, "No woman will ever be able . . ." (Unnamed source found in Ruth Law's biofile, National Air and Space Museum), n.d.

p. 46, "She's an instinctive flier . . ." Adams and Kimball, *Heroines of the Sky,* 52.

p. 50, "A hundred and twenty . . ." *Flying* (December 1916), 454.

p. 50-51, "My flight was done . . ." Moolman, *Women Aloft,* 7.

p. 52, "The real aviator . . ." Obera Rawles, *New York Journal* (May 16, 1936), 7.

p. 54, " I don't care . . ." (Unnamed and undated source found in Ruth Law's biofile, National Air and Space Museum), n.p.

BESSIE COLEMAN

p. 57, "amount to something," Doris Rich, *Queen Bess: Daredevil Aviator* (Washington, DC: Smithsonian Institution Press, 1993), 26.

p. 60, "You just called it . . ." Ibid., 27.

p. 61, "I had thirteen kids . . ." Sheila Turnage, "Claiming the Sky," *American Legacy* (Spring 2000), 22.

p. 64, "We must have aviators . . ." Doris Rich, "My Quest For Queen Bess," *Air & Space* (August/September 1994), 56.

p. 64, "Black Joan of Arc," Audrey Fisher, "Bessie Coleman: Flying in the Face of all Odds," *Woman Pilot* (March/April 1995), 10.

p. 65, "You tell the world . . ." Anita King, *Essence* (June 1976), 48.

p. 65, "Oh, you don't know . . ." Turnage, *American Legacy,* 24.

p. 66, "Bessie Coleman . . ." *Waxahachie Daily Light* (September 25, 1925), n.p.

p. 69, "Lady, didn't your plane . . ." Elois Patterson, *Memoirs of the Late Bessie Coleman Aviatrix, Pioneer of the Negro*

People in Aviation (Privately published by Elois Patterson, 1969), n.p.

p. 69, "I am writing . . ." Turnage, *American Legacy, 26.*

AMELIA EARHART

p. 71, "Books meant much . . ." Amelia Earhart, *The Fun of It* (New York: Brewer, Warren and Putnam, 1932), 6.

p. 72, "A. E.—the girl . . ." Lisa Yount, *Women Aviators* (New York: Facts on File Inc., 1995), 25.

p. 72-73, "I've had twenty-eight . . ." Ibid.

p. 73, "As soon as we left . . ." Dorothy Nathan, *Women of Courage* (New York: Random House, 1964), 120.

p. 77, "Courage is the price . . ." George Putnam, *Soaring Wings: A Biography of Amelia Earhart* (New York: Harcourt, Brace and Company, 1939), 170.

p. 78, "I am at a loss . . ." Earhart, *The Fun of It,* 133.

p. 79, "While I regret . . ." Ibid., 136.

p. 81, "To want in one's heart . . ." Nathan, *Women of Courage,* 132.

p. 81, "A. E.'s personal ambitions . . ." Louise Thaden, *High, Wide and Frightened* (New York: Stackpole Sons, 1938), 259.

p. 84, "I want to do it . . ." Mary Lovell, *The Sound of Wings* (New York: St. Martin's Press, 1989), 2.

RUTH NICHOLS

p. 88, "It seemed as though . . ." Ruth Nichols, *Wings for Life* (New York: L. B. Lippincott Company, 1951), 15.

p. 88, "My heart, however . . ." Ibid., 16.

p. 94, "Thank you, God . . ." Ibid., 191.

p. 95, "Okay, Ruth . . ." Ibid., 193.

p. 95, "RUTH NICHOLS . . ." Ibid., 195.

p. 95, "Get out . . ." Ibid., 197.

p. 97, "Aunty, God did it . . . Ibid.

p. 97, "That Amelia always . . ." Ibid., 100.

p. 98, "In doing so . . ." Planck, *Women With Wings,* 68.

LOUISE THADEN

p. 106, "Hot, salty tears . . ." Thaden, *High, Wide and Frightened,* 40.

p. 107, "This is adventure . . ." Ibid., 71.

p. 107, "I'm away," Ibid., 72.

p. 108, "To us the successful . . ." Ibid., 77.

p. 108, "It is magnificent . . ." Ibid., 82.

p. 109, "I'm glad to be here . . ." Ibid., 89.

p. 109, "If Louise ever . . ." Ibid., 258.

p. 111, "Oh well . . ." Ibid., 120.

p. 113, "Do you know . . ." Ibid., 179.

ANNE MORROW LINDBERGH

p. 120, "Never have I had . . ." Anne Morrow Lindbergh, *Bring Me a Unicorn: Diaries and Letters of Anne Morrow Lindbergh, 1922-1928* (New York: Harcourt Brace Jovanovich, 1972), 232.

p. 120, "He opened the door . . ." Anne Morrow Lindbergh, *Hour of Gold, Hour of Lead: Diaries and Letters of Anne Morrow Lindbergh, 1929-1932* (New York: Brace Jovanovich, 1938), 3.

p. 122, "It was so delicious . . ." Ibid., 126.

p. 125, "I wouldn't take . . ." Anne Morrow Lindbergh, *North to the Orient* (New York: Harcourt, Brace and Company, 1935), 61.

p. 127, "I like everything . . ." Lindbergh, *Hour of Gold, Hour of Lead,* 186.

p. 129, "Ting-miss-ar-tog . . ." Anne Morrow Lindbergh, "Flying Around the North Atlantic," *The National Geographic Magazine* (September 1934), 279.

p. 130, "We shall not cease . . ." Anne Morrow Lindbergh, *Earth Shine* (New York: Harcourt Brace & World, 1969), xiii.

p. 132, "Through the eyes . . ." Ibid., 45.

JACQUELINE COCHRAN

p. 135, "Adventure was always . . ." Jacqueline Cochran and Maryann Brinley, *Jackie Cochran: The Autobiography of the Greatest Woman Pilot in Aviation History* (New York: Bantam Books, 1987), 187.

p. 138, "If you ponder . . ." Ibid., 5.

p. 138, "I just got tired . . ." Claudia Oakes, *United States Women in Aviation, 1930-1939* (Washington, DC: Smithsonian Institution Press, 1985), 35.

p. 142, "Did I have guts," Cochran and Brinley, *Jackie Cochran,* 39.

p. 146, "She was tough . . ." Chuck Yeager, *Yeager* (New York: Bantam Books, 1985), 212.

p. 148, "Adventure is a state . . ." Ibid., 345.

bibliography

Adams, Jean and Margaret Kimball. *Heroines of the Sky.* 2nd ed. Freeport, NY: Books for Libraries Press, 1970.

"Aviatrix Must Sign Away Life to Learn Trade." *Chicago Defender,* October 8, 1921, 2.

Backus, Jean. *Letters From Amelia, 1901-1939.* Boston: Beacon Press, 1982.

"Bessie Coleman, Negro, to Fly here Saturday." *The Waxahachie Daily Light.* September 25, 1925.

Boase, Wendy. *The Sky's the Limit.* New York: MacMillan Publishing Co., 1979.

Brooks-Pazmany, Kathleen. *United States Women in Aviation, 1919-1929.* Washington, DC: Smithsonian Institution Press, 1983.

Buffington, H. Glenn. "The First Women's Air Derby." *American Historical Society Journal* 9 (Fall 1964): 222-224.

Cochran, Jacqueline and Maryann Brinley. *Jackie Cochran: An Autobiography of the Greatest Woman Pilot in Aviation History.* New York: Bantam Books, 1987.

Cochran, Jacqueline. *The Stars at Noon.* Boston: Little, Brown and Co., 1954.

"Colored Aviatrix Bobs Up Again." *Air Service News Letter.* February 20, 1923, 4.

Earhart, Amelia. *The Fun of It.* New York: Brewer, Warren, and Putnam, 1932.

———. (Arranged by George Putnam) *Last Flight.* New York: Harcourt, Brace and World, Inc., 1937.

———. *20 Hrs. 40 Min.* New York: G. P. Putnam's Sons, 1929.

Fischer, Audrey. "Bessie Coleman: Flying in the Face of All

Odds." *Woman Pilot* (March/April 1995): 8-11.

Gee, Henrietta. "Ruth Law, Pioneer Flyer, Had the Courage to Become a Legend." *New York Sun,* July 12, 1932.

Gwynn-Jones, Terry. "For a Brief Moment the World Seemed Wild About Harriet." *Smithsonian,* January 1984.

Holden, Henry and Lori Griffin. *Ladybirds II: The Continuing Story of American Women in Aviation.* Mount Freedom, NJ: Black Hawk Publishing Co., 1993.

Jaros, Dean. *Heroes Without Legacy: American Airwomen 1912-1944.* Niwot, CO: University Press of Colorado, 1993.

"Katherine Stinson Makes a Hit in Flights in Japan." *Billboard,* February 3, 1917.

"Katherine Stinson, The Flying Schoolgirl." *FAA Aviation News* (November 1971): 10-11.

"Katherine Stinson to Fly to Japan." *Billboard,* November 25, 1916).

King, Anita. "Brave Bessie: First Black Pilot, Part II." *Essence,* June 1976.

Lindbergh, Anne Morrow. *Bring Me a Unicorn: Diaries and Letters of Anne Morrow Lindbergh, 1922-1928.* New York: Harcourt Brace Jovanovich, Inc., 1972.

———. *Earth Shine.* Harcourt, Brace & World, 1969.

———. "Flying Around the North Atlantic." *National Geographic Magazine,* September 1934.

———. *Hour of Gold, Hour of Lead: Diaries and Letters of Anne Morrow Lindbergh, 1929-1932.* New York: Harcourt Brace Jovanovich, 1973.

———. *Listen! the Wind.* New York: Harcourt Brace Jovanovich 1938.

———. *North to the Orient.* New York: Harcourt, Brace and Company, 1935.

Lindbergh, Reeve. *No More Words: A Journal of My Mother, Anne Morrow Lindbergh.* New York: Simon & Schuster, 2002.

————. *Under a Wing: A Memoir.* New York: Simon & Schuster, 1998.

Lovell, Mary. *The Sound of Wings.* New York: St. Martin's Press, 1989.

Moolman, Valerie. *Women Aloft.* Alexandria, VA: Time-Life Books, 1981.

Nathan, Dorothy. *Women of Courage.* New York: Random House, 1964.

"Negro Aviatrix." *The Waxahachie Daily Light,* September 22, 1925.

Nichols, Ruth. "Aviation for You and Me." *Ladies Home Journal* (May 1929): 9.

————. "Behind the Ballyhoo." *The American Magazine,* March 1932.

————. *Wings for Life.* Philadelphia: J.P. Lippincott Company, 1957.

————. "You Must Fly" *Pictorial Review,* August 1933.

Oakes, Claudia. *United States Women in Aviation Through World War I.* Washington, DC: Smithsonian Institution Press, 1978.

Patterson, Elois. *Memoirs of the Late Bessie Coleman: Pioneer of the Negro People in Aviation.* Privately published by Elois Patterson, 1969.

Planck, Charles. *Women With Wings.* New York: Harper and Brothers, 1942.

Putnam, George. *Soaring Wings: A Biography of Amelia Earhart.* New York: Harcourt, Brace and Company, 1939.

Quimby, Harriet. "How a Woman Learns to Fly." *Leslie's Illustrated Weekly.* 1911. In Phil's Scott's *The Pioneers of Flight.* Princeton, NJ: Princeton University Press, 1999.

————. "How I Made My First Big Flight Abroad." *Fly Magazine* (June 1912): 8-10.

Rawles, Obera. "'Angel Ruth' Now Reaches for the Moon."

New York Journal, May 16, 1936.

Rich, Doris. *Amelia Earhart: A Biography.* Washington, DC: Smithsonian Institution Press, 1989.

———. "My Quest for Queen Bess." *Air & Space* (August/ September 1994): 54-58.

———. *Queen Bess: Daredevil Aviator.* Washington, DC: Smithsonian Institution Press, 1993.

"Ruth Law Comes Back to Town: Wistfully Recalls Old Flying Days." Unnamed and undated article found in Ruth Law's biofile, National Air and Space Museum.

"Ruth Law, Queen of the Air." *Billboard,* April 24, 1915.

"Ruth Law's Record Breaking Flight." *Flying,* December 1916.

"San Antonio Aviatrix Captures Japan; Katherine Stinson Thrills Nipponese." *San Antonio Express,* January 28, 1917.

Thaden, Louise. *High, Wide and Frightened.* New York: Stackpole Sons, 1938.

———. "The Flying Boudoir." *Air Facts* (April 1968): 59-64.

Turnage, Sheila. "Claiming the Sky." *American Legacy* (Spring 2000): 18-28.

Underwood, John. *The Stinsons.* Glendale, CA: Heritage Press, 1976.

Winegarten, Debra. *Katherine Stinson: The Flying Schoolgirl.* Austin: Eakin Press, 2000.

Yeager, Gen. Chuck and Leo Janes. *Yeager: An Autobiography.* New York: Bantum Books, 1985.

Yount, Lisa. *Women Aviators.* New York: Facts on File Inc., 1995.

web sites

http://www.ninety-nines.org/
With more than 5,000 members, the Ninety-Nines support and encourage women aviators and help keep their history remembered.

http://www.ameliaearhartmuseum.org/
The Amelia Earhart Birthplace Museum features not only a museum devoted to the aviator's life but a one-acre "landscape mural" portrait of Earhart, created with living plants, rocks, and other natural materials.

http://www.firstflight.org/
The First Flight Society was developed to preserve the memory and legacy of the Wright brothers' achievements at Kitty Hawk, North Carolina.

http://www.iwasm.org/
The International Women's Air and Space Museum is dedicated to honoring the history and achievements of women aviators.

http://www.women-in-aviation.com/
A comprehensive site with lots of links, covering all aspects of women in aviation on the Internet.

http://www.nasm.si.edu/
The Smithsonian National Air and Space Museum has wide-ranging exhibits covering all aspects of the topic of flight.

http://www.centennialofflight.gov/index2.cfm
This Web site offers essays about famous fliers, daredevils, and record setters.

index